Academic Vocabulary Building in English

Low-Intermediate

Volume 1

Betsy Davis
Alan Juffs
Dawn E. McCormick
Greg Mizera
M. Christine O'Neill
Stacy Ranson
Missy Slaathaug
Dorolyn Smith

PITT SERIES IN ENGLISH AS A SECOND LANGUAGE

Alan Juffs, Editor

ISBN-13: 978-0-472-03421-5

2018   2017   2016   2015   4   3   2   1

Contents

Introduction to the New Pitt Series in Vocabulary

The importance of the knowledge of vocabulary has been well established in the field of second language teaching and learning in the last ten years and is reflected in both scholarly research and textbooks. In this context, the English Language Institute at the University of Pittsburgh is known for its popular eight-volume series *Words for Students of English* (University of Michigan Press). In the years since the series was first published, we have learned more about how vocabulary is learned and taught (e.g., Coxhead, 2001; Folse, 2004; Hulstijn & Laufer, 2001; Nation, 2001; Paribakt & Wesche, 1997). The faculty at the English Language Institute have been considering new ways to address learners' challenges in acquiring vocabulary. The result of our research and experience is a new series, *Academic Vocabulary Building*. This series weaves together three sets of knowledge: (1) the results of recent research from applied linguists and psycholinguists, (2) the rich classroom experience of the Institute faculty, who together have many decades of practical classroom ESL experience, and (3) the data gathered from our online student database and corpus studies that have informed us of which words students need to know more deeply.

Which Words?

The applied linguistics research on corpora has provided a better idea of which words students need to know (Cobb, www.lextutor.ca; Nation, 2001). In an important study, Coxhead (2001) identified 570 word families in the social sciences and humanities. We focus on those word families in this series because although the 1,000 and 2,000 most frequently occurring words in English account for about 80 percent of words in any text, the 570 academic word list families account for a further 3.9–8.5 percent of words in a newspaper or an academic text. Therefore, if learners know these words, this knowledge will contribute a great deal to their overall comprehension of spoken and written texts.

What Parts of a Word?

What does it mean when we say a student knows a word? Of course, there is much more to knowing a word than its simple form and a meaning or concept. At a minimum, knowing a word means knowledge of its form, meaning, syntax, and morphology. This knowledge also includes register, appropriateness, and cultural content (Levelt, 1989; Nation, 2001). We have, therefore, expanded on form-meaning tasks to include work on the morphology, syntax, and collocations of the words.

Exercises That Teach Vocabulary

Our materials are designed to help students learn all aspects of word structure and meaning. We know that frequency is very important in word learning (Ellis, 2001, 2002), so we have ensured that the words are used in a variety of exercises and forms. We then lead the learner through a process of lexical building that begins with form-meaning recognition, continues through recognition of the internal structure of words, and ends with learner-centered production.

Each unit contains sections that attack various components of word learning. First, each chapter opens with a chart of focus words and their various morphological forms. The chart familiarizes the students with the range of common forms of each word. The next step is the first stage in establishing form-meaning mappings: Each word is listed with a definition, along with two example sentences. In each set of definitions, we present the vocabulary on the theme of the unit and provide at least two morphological variants to begin the morphological input enhancement goals of the series. This step provides the first semantic and syntactic context for each word.

The lists and definitions are followed by exercises that concentrate students' attention on establishing form-meaning links. These exercises consist of practice opportunities that require multiple retrievals to promote label-to-concept links and begin awareness of derivational and inflectional variants. Follow-up exercises focus on collocations, and the final exercise in each chapter is a practice quiz. Additional exercises (available for teachers online) focus on meaning and derivational and inflectional awareness and production.

Several exercises are designed to promote production. Although Folse (2006) has suggested that fill-in-the-blank exercises are more time effective for teachers, others suggest that productive meaning-generating output is essential for deeper learning of vocabulary (Hulstijn & Laufer, 2001), including the involvement load hypothesis, which suggests that deeper processing leads to better learning.

By the time a student has finished a unit, he or she should have had both receptive and productive practice with the form, meaning, morphosyntax, and collocational properties of each lexical item. We hope you find these materials useful, and we look forward to hearing from teachers and learners who use the books.

Alan Juffs
Director, English Language Institute
Pittsburgh, 2015

References

Coxhead, A. (2001). A new academic word list. *TESOL Quarterly, 34*, 213–238.

Ellis, N. C. (2001). Memory for language. In P. Robinson (Ed.), *Cognition and second language instruction* (pp. 33–68). New York: Cambridge University Press.

Ellis, N. C. (2002). Frequency effects in language processing. *Studies in Second Language Acquisition 24*(2), 143–188.

Folse, K. S. (2004). *Vocabulary myths: Applying second language research to classroom teaching.* Ann Arbor: University of Michigan Press.

Folse, K. S. (2006). The effect of type of written exercise on L2 vocabulary retention. *TESOL Quarterly, 40*, 273–293.

Hulstijn, J., & Laufer, B. (2001). Some empirical evidence for the involvement load hypothesis in vocabulary acquisition. *Language Learning, 51*, 539–558.

Levelt, W. (1989). *Speaking: From intention to articulation.* Cambridge: MIT Press.

Nation, I. S. P. (2001). *Learning vocabulary in another language.* Cambridge, U.K.: Cambridge University Press.

Paribakht, T.S., & M. Wesche (1997). Vocabulary enhancement activities and reading for meaning in second language vocabulary acquisition. In J. Coady and T. Huckin (Eds.), *Second language vocabulary acquisition* (pp. 174–200). Cambridge, U.K.: Cambridge University Press.

Scope and Sequence

Volume 1

Unit 1 Business	Unit 2 Health	Unit 3 Sports	Unit 4 Transportation	Unit 5 Fashion and Design	Unit 6 Food and Nutrition	Unit 7 Plants and Animals	Unit 8 Science
Vocabulary Practice							
A. Match Point (R – M)	A. Make the Connection (R – M)	A. Make the Connection (R – M)	A. Make the Connection (R – M)	A. Match Point (R – M)	A. Make the Connection (R – M)	A. Match Point (R – M)	A. Make the Connection (R – M)
B. Branching Out (R – F)	B. Branching Out (R – F)	B. What's the Word? (P – F/M)	B. Branching Out (R – F)	B. In the Wrong Place (R – M)	B. Switch It Up (R – F)	B. Make the Connection (R – M)	B. Switch It Up (R – F)
C. In the Wrong Place (R – M)	C. Off Base (P – F)	C. Off Base (P – F)	C. Off Base (P – F)	C. What's the Word? (P – F/M)	C. In the Wrong Place (R – M)	C. Switch It Up (R – F)	C. In the Wrong Place (R – M)
D. What's the Word? (P – F/M)	D. What's the Word? (P – F/M)	D. In the Wrong Place (R – M)	D. What's Missing? (P – F/M)	D. Off Base (P – F)	D. What's the Word? (P – F/M)	D. Off Base (P – F)	D. What's the Word? (P – F/M)
Frequent Collocations							
E. Complete the Thought (P – F)	E. Not Meant To Be (R – M)	E. Balancing Act (P – F)	E. Not Meant To Be (R – M)	E. Balancing Act (P – F)	E. Get It Together (R – M)	E. Not Meant To Be (R – M)	E. Not Meant To Be (R – M)
F. Get It Together (P – M)	F. Complete the Thought (P – F)	F. Get It Together (P – M)	F. Get It Together (P – M)	F. Complete the Thought (P – F)	F. Not Meant To Be (R – M)	F. Stick Like Glue (R – F)	F. Get It Together (R – M)
Practice Quiz							
G. The Choice Is Yours (R – F/M)	G. The Choice Is Yours (R – F/M)	G. The Choice Is Yours (R – F/M)	G. The Choice Is Yours (R – F/M)	G. The Choice Is Yours (R – F/M)	G. The Choice Is Yours (R – F/M)	G. The Choice Is Yours (R – F/M)	G. The Choice Is Yours (R – F/M)
H. Sense or Nonsense? (R – F/M)	H. Sense or Nonsense? (R – F/M)	H. Sense or Nonsense? (R – F/M)	H. Sense or Nonsense? (R – F/M)	H. Sense or Nonsense? (R – F/M)	H. Sense or Nonsense? (R – F/M)	H. Sense or Nonsense? (R – F/M)	H. Sense or Nonsense? (R – F/M)

Key: R = Receptive, P = Productive, F = Form, M = Meaning

To the Teacher

Word Form Chart

The word forms included in the chart present students with their first contact with different forms that are possible and frequent for each word. However, a word may not have been included because it is not used frequently enough to be relevant to students at this level. Teachers should review it, asking students to recognize which words have only noun forms, which have verb forms, and which have adjective forms that contain suffixes, etc. The form in bold represents the primary form defined/taught in the unit. Often, this is the more frequent form that students will encounter.

The words were cross-checked in two dictionaries (*Longman Dictionary of American English* and *Cambridge English Dictionary*) to be sure that only the most frequent and useful forms were included.

Definitions and Examples of Word Forms

Definitions and examples are given for each word to further the recognition of forms that students are exposed to, as well as to introduce meanings of each word and contexts the word is frequently used in. Since each unit has a theme, the meanings and contexts are also limited to the ones that correspond to the theme.

Vocabulary Practice

Vocabulary Practice includes exercises focused on recognizing the meanings of words and their forms. Exercises require students to work with forms and meanings at the word level. You may want students to do these exercises in pairs or individually in class after studying the Word Form Chart and Definitions and Examples section as homework.

- **Branching Out** helps students focus on the forms of the word—both morphological (noun, verb, adjective, adverb) and derivational (present, past). The Word Form Chart should be consulted if students don't know the forms yet. In this way, they will be processing the information while working at a fairly easy level.
- **In the Wrong Place** focuses on the meaning of each word. While the number of possible answer choices is limited, each word has to be evaluated in each possible blank. Extended paragraph contexts give more information about meaning.
- **Make the Connection** asks students to match a word from the list to a suitable context.
- **Match Point** requires students to match broad meanings or examples to a given form of the word.

- **Off Base** requires students to replace a word or phrase in each sentence with its antonym from the Word Form Chart. This exercise requires that students understand the meaning of the word and that they use the correct form of the word. It also exposes students to another example of how the word is used.
- **Switch It Up** asks students to correct the form of the word given in a sentence. The Word Form Chart may be consulted if students cannot remember the form. Students may need help analyzing the sentences to determine which form is needed.
- **What's the Word?** allows students to synthesize the form/meaning/ use connection. The idea is that students use their memories to create the clues. This requirement allows the information to be practiced productively.
- **What's Missing?** presents paragraphs into which words from a list must be inserted. This activity requires knowledge of both form and meaning.

Frequent Collocations

Collocations are fixed expressions that are frequently used by native speakers. Such terms as *crystal clear, middle management, nuclear family,* and *cosmetic surgery* are examples of collocated pairs of words. Knowing which words are frequently used together is important for students since even if a student uses the correct grammar, a sentence may sound awkward if the wrong words are used together; for example, a student may use *forceful coffee* instead of *strong coffee.* The collocations listed are **some of** the most frequent ones found in Brigham Young University's Corpus of Contemporary American English (COCA) but are primarily limited to those that are suitable **only** to the context of each unit. In other words, the lists in each unit are not meant to be exhaustive or to include common phrases **not** related to the unit theme. Exercises focus on connecting the unit vocabulary words with possible collocates alone and in example sentences.

- **Balancing Act** asks the student to retrieve the collocate or unit vocabulary word that is missing in a given phrase.
- **Complete the Thought** assumes the student can retrieve the collocate or unit vocabulary word that is missing in a complete sentence.
- **Get It Together** provides examples of collocations within sentences that students are required to unscramble and rewrite. This gives them another example in an appropriate context. Clues are offered to get students started.
- **Not Meant To Be** requires students to match a word and its collocate, which helps students memorize the list.
- **Stick Like Glue** asks students to recognize which words from a word bank are commonly used with specific unit vocabulary.

Practice Quiz

- **The Choice Is Yours** is a multiple choice exercise that tests whether students have learned the meanings of the words.
- **Sense or Nonsense?** is a true or false exercise that focuses on the correct use of the words in context.

Unit 1

Business

Word Form Chart

Noun	Verb	Adjective	Adverb
acquisition	acquire		
asset			
briefing brief	**brief**		
capital capitalism	capitalize		
compensation	**compensate** **compensate for**		
compromise	compromise		
conduct	**conduct**		
deduction	**deduct**		
export	**export**		
founding	**found**	founded well-founded	
incentive	incentivize		
investment	**invest**		
relevance		**irrelevant** relevant	irrelevantly
mutual		**mutual**	mutually
optimism optimist	optimize	**optimistic**	optimistically
personnel		personnel	
specification	**specify**	specific	specifically
violation violator	**violate**		

Definitions and Examples of Word Forms

1. **acquisition,** n., something that you get; buying or taking over a company

   When your business grows, <u>acquisition</u> of your competitor is one way to improve your share of the market.

   Companies try to make sure they are successful by buying new equipment. For example, a moving company might <u>acquire</u> (v.t.) new trucks every three years.

2. **asset,** n., something valuable that is owned by an individual, group, or corporation

   A company's <u>assets</u> include offices, factories, and also investments and personnel.

   At the meeting, the directors of the Tenex Corporation decided to sell off some of its <u>assets</u> in order to raise some cash.

3. **brief,** v.t., to give a summary or short report to someone

   At the yearly meeting, the finance director <u>briefs</u> company shareholders on income and costs.

   The chief executive officer will hold a <u>briefing</u> (n.) for the other directors so they can set goals for the future.

4. **capital,** n., the money used to begin and support a business

   Companies can create <u>capital</u> by selling property or stock.

   A good businessperson tries to <u>capitalize</u> (v.i.) on the opportunities that arise.

5a.   compensate, v.t., to pay a person or organization for work

Managers are usually <u>compensated</u> more than manual workers because they are responsible for many parts of the business.

A company provides different levels of <u>compensation</u> (n.), depending on the roles of people in the organization and their responsibilities.

5b.   compensate for, v., to balance something negative with something positive

Five more vacation days do not <u>compensate</u> employees <u>for</u> all the money lost on benefits.

In <u>compensation</u> (n.) <u>for</u> the benefits that were cut, workers were allowed five more vacation days a year.

6.   compromise, n., an agreement that requires each party to give up something

Group members often have to make <u>compromises</u> to reach a decision.

During negotiations, managers and workers usually <u>compromise</u> (v.t.) on issues such as wages and benefits.

7a.   conduct, v.t., to behave in a certain way

When college graduates start to work for a company, they must <u>conduct</u> themselves in a more serious way than they did during college.

7b.   conduct, v.t., to carry out a formal process

The company <u>conducted</u> a search for a new branch manager.

8. **deduct**, v.t., to take away from, subtract

   In order to calculate how much profit a company makes, you must <u>deduct</u> costs from income.

   The salary that a person takes home is the money left after <u>deductions</u> (n.) for health care, retirement, and taxes.

9. **export**, v.t., to send products or services to another country

   Countries in the Middle East have <u>exported</u> oil all over the world.

   Financial services are an important <u>export</u> (n.) for developed countries.

10. **found**, v.t., to create a company or other organization

    Sam Watson <u>founded</u> the MicroPro Company in Houston.

    A lot of time is spent carefully planning a newly <u>founded</u> (adj.) enterprise.

11. **incentive**, n., a reward to encourage someone to do something

    A big <u>incentive</u> for employees who work harder than others is an increased level of pay.

    People need <u>incentives</u> such as promotion to a higher position if they are expected to take on more responsibility.

12. **invest**, v.t., to buy assets in the hope that their value will increase

    Many people <u>invest</u> in the stock market to save for retirement.

    There are many kinds of <u>investments</u> (n.), including the buying of gold and real estate, as well as placing money in interest-bearing accounts in banks.

13. **irrelevant**, adj., not related to, or having nothing to do with, a subject

The skill of managers is <u>irrelevant</u> when the demand for a product disappears.

National borders are not <u>relevant</u> when talking about the global economy because many large companies have factories all over the world.

14. **mutual**, adj., something that is shared or done together

A <u>mutual</u> fund is an investment tool that shares risk over different stocks, bonds, and cash.

A contract to buy a house is signed when the buyer and the seller <u>mutually</u> (adv.) agree on the price.

15. **optimistic**, adj., having a good or positive attitude about the future

After many months of decline in value, some economists are <u>optimistic</u> about the future of the dollar.

Jake is an <u>optimist</u> (n.) because he believes that new technologies will solve the climate change problem.

16. **personnel**, n., the people who work for a company or organization (usually takes a plural verb)

<u>Personnel</u>, sometimes called "human capital," are a valuable asset of any company.

The <u>personnel</u> (adj.) department is responsible for processing paychecks, administering insurance plans, and hiring employees.

17. **specify,** v.t., to give detailed information about something; to be exact or precise

    The Holiday Toy Company <u>specified</u> that the new doll had to be introduced two months before the holiday season.

    Computer parts must be made according to exact <u>specifications</u> (n.) in order to function correctly.

18. **violate,** v.t., to break a rule or a law

    In the future, car manufacturers will not be able to <u>violate</u> strict limits on pollution.

    If a U.S. company sold advanced military technology to a foreign country, it would be a <u>violation</u> (n.) of U.S. export controls.

Vocabulary Practice

A. Match Point

Write the letter of the best definition next to each word. The first one has been done as an example.

1. __d__   violate   a. the people who work in a company

2. _____   specify   b. to begin a new business or organization

3. _____   personnel   c. to gain by either buying, trading, or learning

4. _____   optimism   d̸. to not follow a rule or law

5. _____   mutual   e. to say exactly what a procedure or product should be

6. _____   invest   f. opposite of add

7. _____   incentive   g. when both sides have something in common

8. _____   found   h. agreement made when each side is flexible

9. _____   deduct   i. to use your money to earn a profit

10. _____   compromise   j. anything of value that you have

11. _____   asset   k. a person's positive outlook

12. _____   acquire   l. prize for doing something better than before

B. Branching Out

Write the correct form of the word. Refer to the Word Form Chart if necessary. You may have to change the verb form. The first one has been done as an example.

1. **acquire**

   a. By _____*acquiring*_____ new technology, businesses can improve efficiency.

   b. The management team of Big Business Corporation decided to _____ a new computer and software.

   c. It is clear that the _____ of technology is important to Big Business Corporation.

2. **found**

   a. Jim Evans _____ his company, General Business, in Mexico in the late 1970s.

   b. Other business people collect money from investors before they can _____ a company.

   c. The _____ of a business or a company takes time, money, and hard work.

3. **invest**

   a. Mary always _____ in a variety of companies to reduce her risk of losing money.

   b. Another _____ that some people choose is government bonds.

   c. How to _____ for early retirement interests many people.

4. **compromise**

   a. The managers and the workers _____ on work conditions for a special project last week.

   b. The managers reached a _____ with the workers on the pay level for overtime.

   c. In a negotiation, everyone has to _____ on something.

5. **deduction**

   a. When paying federal taxes in the United States, you can make several _____ from your income to reduce your taxes.

   b. It is possible to _____ some business expenses if your company has not paid you for them.

   c. Don't forget that you can _____ donations that you make to charities from you taxes.

6. **brief**

    a. A good _____ should be short, but it should contain specific and useful information.

    b. One responsibility of an executive is to _____ managers and workers about business conditions.

    c. On the other hand, senior workers should provide some type of _____ to managers on the difficulties they found in manufacturing.

C. In the Wrong Place

In each paragraph, the underlined vocabulary words are in the wrong place. Cross out the inappropriate word and replace it with the underlined word that makes sense. The first one has been done as an example.

1. Globalization is an important force in the world economy. Leaders in the car industry, the food industry, and the credit card industry have ~~exported~~ _**acquired**_ companies from several countries. As a result, jobs are being ~~acquired~~ _**exported**_ from industrialized countries to developing countries.

2. Several conditions must be met before a company can compromise_____ international business. One condition is having enough start-up money. Investors can provide violate_____ for companies to enter new markets. In addition, international trade may require countries to capital_____ on taxes in order to attract new businesses. However, companies should not conduct_____ trade agreements if they want to have successful relationships with a country.

3. In any business, the amount of <u>irrelevant</u> _____ is an
    important question. Decisions have to be made about basic pay and
    additional <u>personnel</u> _____ for excellent work. Pay raises
    may depend on <u>incentives</u> _____ performance, but should not
    be based on <u>compensation</u> _____ factors such as age, gender,
    or race.

4. Jamesco is a small business run by an individual in a small town.
    The owner, Jim Banes, needs to give his employees a
    <u>conduct</u> _____ on the state of the business occasionally.
    Jim tells them about the company's <u>capitalize</u> _____
    and how their <u>assets</u> _____ affects the company's
    bottom line. Finally, Jim coaches them about how to
    <u>briefing</u> _____ on client meetings in order to
    increase profits.

5. Having an export business is not easy, as Xin is finding out. First of all,
    in order to <u>violation</u> _____ his business, he needs to find
    ways to increase sales. When he increases the amount of product he sells,
    he wants to be sure his <u>specifications</u> _____ is safe. He has
    to make sure the <u>optimize</u> _____ are acceptable to the
    overseas shippers so he doesn't waste any money. The final step is to be
    sure there is no <u>investment</u> _____ of international trade laws
    so that he doesn't receive any sanctions or fines.

D. What's the Word?

With your partner, fill in each box on the grid. Student A will use Grid A. Student B will use Grid B in Appendix 1 on page 165. Each grid is missing different words. Describe the words on your grid so your partner can fill in his or her blank spaces. When all of the blanks are full, compare your grids to see if you have the correct answers.

> **Example:** For Box 1, Student A might give Student B these clues: *It's a verb. It's when you learn a new skill. It means to make a large purchase in a formal way.*

Grid A

1 acquire	5	9 optimist	13
2	6 brief	10	14 found
3 irrelevant	7	11 asset	15 personnel
4	8 capitalism	12	16

Frequent Collocations: Business

Collocations are fixed expressions that are frequently used by native speakers. Knowing which words are frequently used together is important because your sentence may sound awkward if the wrong words are used together.

Correct: *crystal clear, middle management, nuclear family, cosmetic surgery*

Incorrect: *diamond clear, middle supervisor, ~~restricted family~~, cosmetic operation*

Some common business collocations are listed. What others can you think of?

1. **acquisition**—acquisition of knowledge or skills, mergers and acquisitions, a million dollar acquisition
2. **asset**—asset management, a financial asset, a valuable asset
3. **capital**—capital gains, a capital investment, venture capital
4. **compensate**—executive compensation, worker's compensation, to compensate for
5. **conduct**—to conduct business, criminal conduct, professional conduct
6. **found**—to found a company, to found a group, to go on to found [a company]
7. **incentive**—financial incentive, little/much incentive, to provide incentive
8. **invest**—foreign investment, investment firm, to invest in companies
9. **optimistic**—to be cautiously optimistic, to be optimistic about, a sense of optimism
10. **violate**—to violate a law, to violate someone's rights, to violate someone's privacy

E. Complete the Thought

Complete each sentence by filling in the blank with a missing part of a collocation from the unit. (The given part of the collocation is underlined.) The first one has been done as an example.

1. Canco Company wishes to buy an overseas factory that will be a million dollar _acquisition_ .

2. After a year of good sales in the auto industry, large car manufacturing companies are fairly _____ about next year.

3. One method that managers use to improve productivity is to provide workers with _____ such as extra time off to get workers to work faster.

4. When a company has been in business for a long time, the buildings and equipment get old and worn out. It is then necessary to make a capital _____ in new infrastructure.

5. Ravi needs help investing his money since he has a very successful new business, so he found an _____ management firm to help him.

6. Companies with foreign investments must be careful not to _____ a law overseas.

7. Jerszy Luckowitz _____ an internet company when he was only 12 years old.

8. The head of Boston Oil Company was found guilty of criminal _____ and fined 2.5 billion dollars.

F. Get It Together

Unscramble the words and phrases to write sentences containing the collocations. The first one has been done as an example.

1. Sexual harassment / a person's rights / violates

   <u>Sexual harassment violates a person's rights.</u>

2. often go on / new companies / Successful / to found / businesswomen

   _____

   _____

3. to maintain / It is important / with customers / professional conduct / and co-workers

   _____

   _____

4. extra hours / are unhappy / compensate fairly for / Workers / because / the company does not

   _____

   _____

5. an online jewelry store / to start / capital / venture / Sharon needed

_____

_____

6. thought that / Joe / there was / incentive / to work / little / extra hours / for him

_____

_____

7. violates / If a manager / a subordinate's rights, / he or she / will be fired

_____

_____

8. cautiously / that the economy / Businesses are / is improving / optimistic

_____

_____

Practice Quiz

G. The Choice Is Yours

Circle the best answer.

1. A violation of international trading laws would _____.

    a. produce a profit for the company

    b. be considered good luck

    c. cause the company to lose business

    d. be punished by a fine or a jail sentence

2. An import-export business is an example of _____.

    a. a management plan

    b. a government policy

    c. an international trading company

    d. the length/width/cost of a product

3. An overly optimistic person is someone who _____.

    a. frequently makes business decisions

    b. always thinks the best result will occur

    c. always receives mutual benefits

    d. can see the dangers in founding a new business

4. Capital is ____.

    a. the amount of money a business earns

    b. the buildings and personnel in a company

    c. the most important city in the state of Venture

    d. money from investors to support a new business

5. If management and the work force agree to a compromise, then ____.

    a. both sides agree to give up some demands

    b. the management gives in to the workers

    c. the workers give in to the management

    d. they do not reach an agreement

6. It is illegal for a stock broker to ____.

    a. invest in another company

    b. carry out import-export trade

    c. exchange hours with another employee

    d. use insider information to buy or sell stocks and shares

7. When two companies both gain an advantage through their cooperation, then the arrangement is ____.

    a. overly optimistic

    b. seemingly irrelevant

    c. mutually beneficial

    d. confidentially brief

8. Adequate compensation is _____.

    a. enough money for the job

    b. not enough money for the job

    c. too much money for the job

    d. an unfair amount of money for the job

9. A confidential briefing should _____.

    a. not be discussed with people outside the meeting

    b. be announced publicly on television

    c. not be kept a secret from the whole company

    d. be punished with a ten-year jail sentence

10. If clients provide precise specifications on a product, then _____.

    a. they give the manufacturer a wide range of choices

    b. they give the manufacturer exact details about it

    c. they have no preferences about it

    d. they dislike the manufacturer's proposals

H. Sense or Nonsense?

Using your knowledge of the unit's target vocabulary, write Y (yes) for statements that make sense or N (no) for statements that do not make sense.

1. _____ Department heads may use extra pay as an incentive for the sales staff.

2. _____ It is impossible for one company to acquire another.

3. _____ The Microsoft Corporation was founded in 1900.

4. _____ Asset management involves careful supervision of workers' safety.

5. _____ A company will usually deduct taxes before a worker receives his or her salary.

6. _____ The company expects honest conduct from its chief financial officer.

7. _____ Laborers frequently brief the executives in a company.

8. _____ The government is irrelevant to the economy and business profits.

9. _____ An optimistic sales team is beneficial to the company.

10. _____ Individuals can invest their money to make a profit.

Unit 2

Health

Word Form Chart

Noun	Verb	Adjective	Adverb
allergy allergen		allergic	
diagnosis diagnostic	**diagnose**	diagnostic	
epidemic		epidemic	
fatality		**fatal**	fatally
grief	grieve	grieving	
healing healer	**heal**		
infection	infect	infected infectious	
injection	inject		
menace	menace	menacing	menacingly
mood moodiness		moody	moodily
mortality		**mortal**	mortally
recurrence	**recur**	recurring recurrent	
sibling			
sympathy sympathizer	**sympathize**	sympathetic	sympathetically
symptom		symptomatic	
vision	visualize	visual	visually
wound	wound	wounded	

Definitions and Examples of Word Forms

1. **allergy,** n., an illness or reaction caused by coming into contact with something in the environment

    People who have an <u>allergy</u> to peanuts can become sick if they eat something that has been in contact with peanuts. Their throats may swell up and they may have trouble breathing.

    A lot of people are <u>allergic</u> (adj.) to cats; they sneeze and their eyes become red and itchy if they are in a room with cats.

2. **diagnose,** v.t., to determine the cause of a health problem

    Dan had headaches for several months before he was <u>diagnosed</u> with a brain tumor.

    One <u>diagnostic</u> (adj.) test that the average person can do to check for stroke is to ask the person to walk in a straight line. If he or she cannot do this, call for emergency medical assistance immediately.

3. **epidemic,** n., an illness or a disease that happens in a large number of people at the same time

    The great influenza <u>epidemic</u> of 1918–1919 killed more than 50,000,000 people around the world.

    Ebola has affected so many people that scientists now consider it an <u>epidemic</u>.

4. **fatal,** adj., resulting in or causing death

Li Min's brother Tang was in a very serious car accident, but fortunately his injuries were not <u>fatal</u>. He had many broken bones but he recovered in a year.

Today, <u>fatalities</u> (n.) from diseases such as tuberculosis or pneumonia are rare because we have antibiotics that can cure them.

5. **grief,** n., a feeling of great sadness at the death of someone or at the loss of something important in one's life

The display of <u>grief</u> by the people of Britain at the death of Princess Diana included leaving flowers and messages at the gates of Buckingham Palace.

People <u>grieve</u> (v.i.) in different ways; some people <u>grieve</u> internally and quietly, while others are more open about it.

6. **heal,** v.i., to recover from an injury

A broken bone can take six to eight weeks to <u>heal</u>. This is the time that is needed for the bone to grow back together completely.

When my grandmother was <u>healing</u> from heart surgery, she developed an infection.

7. **infection,** n., illness caused by bacteria or a virus

If a cut or an injury is not cleaned properly, it may not heal. The first sign of an <u>infection</u> is that the injury becomes red and swollen.

During the winter in the Northern Hemisphere, you must take good care of your health to avoid becoming <u>infected</u> (adj.) with the flu.

8. **injection**, n., a way of putting medicine or a drug into a person's body by using a needle

   Children are usually afraid of getting <u>injections</u> from the doctor because the needle can cause pain.

   Drug addicts who <u>inject</u> (v.t.) heroin run the risk of becoming infected with AIDS if they share needles with other addicts.

9. **menace**, n., a threat or danger

   Poor waste removal is a <u>menace</u> to society. For example, dirty and diseased conditions were the leading cause of typhoid in Europe and America during the nineteenth century.

   When Jamie was seven years old, he developed a fear of needles because the large needle his doctor used looked so <u>menacing</u> (adj.).

10. **mood**, n., a person's feeling at any particular time, usually temporary

    Mr. Chandra didn't like doctors, and his <u>mood</u> changed whenever he had to go to the doctor's office.

    I don't like taking decongestants because they make me too <u>moody</u> (adj.).

11. **mortal**, adj., not able to live forever

    All human beings and animals are <u>mortal</u>. Some people will die of old age, some of disease, and some of accidents or murder.

    My mother's heart attack at the age of 76 forced me to recognize her <u>mortality</u> (n.).

12. **recur,** v.i., when an illness or disease occurs again

Ivan was declared free of lymphoma after his chemotherapy treatments. Unfortunately, the cancer <u>recurred</u> after several years, and he died of the disease.

Polio almost disappeared from the earth by the 1990s, but there has been a <u>recurrence</u> (n.) of it recently in parts of Africa and Asia.

13. **sibling,** n., brother or sister

Jana's two <u>siblings</u>, one brother and one sister, are both doctors.

Because <u>siblings</u> are so closely related, they may share similar health problems, especially diseases such as diabetes that have a genetic basis.

14. **sympathize,** v.t., to feel sorry for someone who has experienced something bad

As a teacher, Felipe cannot <u>sympathize</u> with a student who has failed his class unless he or she missed class due to illness.

The president extended his <u>sympathy</u> (n.) to the families of the soldiers wounded in action.

15. **symptom,** n., a physical sign in the body that is common in a particular illness or disease

One <u>symptom</u> of a heart attack is the feeling of pain or weakness in the left arm or side of the face.

Being thirsty all the time can indicate someone is <u>symptomatic</u> (adj.) of diabetes.

16. **vision,** n., the ability to see; to see in the mind

> Everyone's eyes get weaker as they get older, so many people who have always had good <u>vision</u> need glasses to read by the time they are in their late 40s.

> Jalal was born with the ability to see, so after he went blind at the age of 15, he was still able to <u>visualize</u> (v.t.) his surroundings.

17. **wound,** n., an injury or cut to the skin, usually caused by a strong force or an intentional attack

> A policeman in our town was attacked by a man with a knife. Fortunately, the <u>wound</u> was not deep.

> Many soldiers and civilians were mortally <u>wounded</u> (v.t.) in the war in Iraq from roadside bombs.

Vocabulary Practice

A. Make the Connection

Choose the vocabulary word that is most closely related to each sentence. The first one has been done as an example.

diagnose	fatal	epidemic
heal	siblings	~~allergy~~
infection	vision	grief

1. The pollen produced by grasses and flowers in the spring and fall cause people to cough and sneeze. _____ *allergy* _____

2. Sometimes there are many people who get the same illness, and it is difficult to care for so many of them at the same time.

   _____

3. The skin becomes red and inflamed after bacteria gets into a cut.

   _____

4. Some illnesses can affect your ability to see clearly.

   _____

5. You do this when you start to feel better from an illness or infection.

   _____

6. Some people do not recover from serious diseases and they die.

   _____

7. Brothers and sisters may have the same genetic defects because they are closely related. _____

8. It is easy to look up information on the internet, but you really need a professional to tell you exactly what is wrong with you.

   _____

9. When someone close to you dies, you feel sadness and pain for a period of time afterward. _____

B. Branching Out

Write the correct form of the word. Refer to the Word Form Chart if necessary.
You may have to change the verb form. The first one has been done as an
example.

1. **diagnose**

    a. Will the doctor _____*diagnose*_____ the patient's illness as a heart
       attack?

    b. His initial _____ was that the patient had an ulcer.

    c. However, the _____ exams that were performed
       showed that the patient had something more serious than an ulcer.

2. **inject**

    a. When Jack went to Cambodia, his doctor _____
       him with a vaccine against hepatitis.

    b. He received two _____ to be fully protected against
       the disease.

    c. He was sorry that the hepatitis vaccine is only available as an
       _____ and not as a pill.

3. **sympathy**

   a. I have a cousin who always seems to understand me. No matter what the problem is, she always speaks _____ to me.

   b. For example, she _____ with me when I was trying to quit smoking. She said she knew that it was a difficult thing to do because she had done it herself.

   c. She expressed her _____ about my grandmother's death by sending me flowers.

4. **grief**

   a. When Fatimah's son died, her _____ was so strong that she didn't think she could continue living.

   b. She _____ so much that she had trouble getting up in the morning.

   c. This _____ mother found that after a few years her pain had decreased and she could smile again.

5. **recur**

   a. Some diseases that had almost disappeared in the last 30 to 50 years
       have _____ recently.

   b. For example, rickets is a children's disease caused by a lack of
       Vitamin D from sunshine. There has been a _____
       of rickets in the United States and Australia because people are not
       getting enough sunshine because of the fear of skin cancer.

   c. The last great bubonic plague epidemic took place in the late 1800s.
       However, approximately 1,700 individual cases of the plague
       _____ every year around the world.

6. **wound**

   a. Samantha was working in the U.S. Federal Building in Oklahoma
       City when it was bombed in 1995. She was _____
       when a piece of pipe from the explosion cut her leg.

   b. The _____ was deep and required surgery.

   c. Fortunately, doctors were able to save the _____
       leg.

7. **visual**

   a. Thabo is _____ disabled as a result of an
       accident when he was two years old. He was playing with fireworks
       when they exploded in his face.

   b. He completely lost the _____ in his left eye.

   c. However, as an architect, he can still _____
       a new hospital on the land where an old steel mill used to be.

C. Off Base

The underlined word in each sentence does not make sense. Cross out each underlined word or phrase, and replace it with a vocabulary word from the unit that fits the context. You may have to change the verb form. The first one has been done as an example.

1. I used to have excellent ~~hearing~~ _vision_ but now I have to wear reading glasses.

2. The scar from Betsy's knee surgery <u>got worse</u> _____ in only a few weeks. You could hardly see it after a few months.

3. Unfortunately, Larry's cancer <u>happened only once</u> _____ despite the chemotherapy and other treatments that he received.

4. Some very strong infections, such as MRSA, require a strong antibiotic. The antibiotic must be <u>swallowed</u> _____; it cannot be taken as a pill.

5. One of the hardest parts of a doctor's job is to have to tell family members that their loved one's illness or accident has been <u>life-saving</u> _____.

6. AIDS has been a/an <u>non-threatening</u> _____ disease that has left up to 12 percent of the children in sub-Saharan Africa without parents.

7. In Europe, there has been a/an <u>small number</u> _____ of
   E. coli infections.

8. After a major disaster like Hurricane Katrina, the survivors have no time
   to <u>celebrate</u> _____ their losses because they have to find
   food and shelter.

9. Most people <u>don't care</u> _____ with others who have
   suffered an accident.

10. Marc's <u>parents</u> _____ were younger than he was, so he
    had to take care of them when they were sick.

D. What's the Word?

With your partner, fill in each box on the grid. Student A will use Grid A. Student B will use Grid B in Appendix 1 on page 166. Each grid is missing different words. Describe the words on your grid so your partner can fill in his or her blank spaces. When all of the blanks are full, compare your grids to see if you have the correct answers.

> **Example:** For Box 1, Student A might give Student B these clues: *It's a verb. To feel extremely sad. You do this when someone in your family dies.*

Grid A

1 grieve	5	9 diagnose	13
2	6 visually	10	14 sympathize
3 wounded	7	11 recurrence	15
4	8 injection	12	16 moodiness

Frequent Collocations: Health

Some common health collocations are listed. What others can you think of?

1. **epidemic**—an AIDS epidemic, an obesity epidemic, of epidemic proportions
2. **fatal**—potentially fatal, a fatal accident, a fatal disease
3. **heal**—to heal itself, to heal wounds, to help heal
4. **infection**—a bacterial infection, a risk of infection, an HIV infection
5. **injection**—a drug injection, a lethal injection, an injection site
6. **mood**—mood swings, to be in a bad/good mood
7. **mortal**—infant mortality, mortal wound, a mortality rate, mortality and morbidity
8. **sympathize**—to have/feel sympathy for, to have/feel little sympathy for, to sympathize with
9. **vision**—peripheral vision, vision loss, a visual impairment
10. **wound**—a gunshot/bullet wound, to be mortally wounded, to be seriously wounded

E. Not Meant To Be

These collocations are incorrect. Read all of the underlined words, and choose the one that best matches or collocates with the first word. Use the list of frequent collocations to help you. The first one has been done as an example.

1. ~~seriously~~ <u>vision</u>   *seriously wounded* _____

2. bad <u>mortality</u>   _____

3. drug ~~wounded~~   _____

4. risk of <u>for</u>   _____

5. infant <u>disease</u>   _____

6. fatal <u>mood</u>   _____

7. peripheral <u>infection</u>   _____

8. sympathy <u>injection</u>   _____

F. Complete the Thought

Fill in the blank in each collocation with a unit vocabulary word. The first one has been done as an example.

1. The AIDS_____*epidemic*_____ is spread by the use of dirty needles, among other factors.

2. IEDs in war zones mortally _____ many soldiers.

3. A high fever may be the first sign of a bacterial _____.

4. My mother had _____ loss for several weeks after her cataract surgery.

5. The nurse's skill helped _____ Jin's anxiety quickly.

6. Tom stopped taking the antibiotic because it caused _____ swings.

7. Although the flu is a common illness, it is potentially _____ in elderly people.

8. Cover the _____ site with a bandage to stop the bleeding.

Practice Quiz

G. The Choice Is Yours

Circle the best answer.

1. If there is an influenza epidemic, it means that _____.

   a. a few people have become sick with influenza

   b. influenza still exists but it doesn't make anyone sick

   c. many people have become sick with influenza

   d. influenza has disappeared

2. A man who is fatally injured will _____.

   a. get better from his injuries and probably live a long life

   b. be a danger to people near him

   c. not feel the effects of his injuries

   d. die from his injuries

3. An infection is _____.

   a. caused by a virus or bacteria

   b. a way to receive medicine through a needle

   c. a type of wound

   d. a disease like cancer

4. If I have two siblings, it means that _____.

   a. I have two sisters

   b. I have two brothers

   c. I have a brother and a sister

   d. I have either two sisters, two brothers, or a sister and a brother

5. A menacing disease is a disease that _____.

   a. kills everyone

   b. is not dangerous to most people

   c. is threatening to many people

   d. has disappeared

6. A wounded person has probably been hurt with _____.

   a. bad food

   b. a knife

   c. an infection

   d. an allergy

7. A person who is suffering from grief probably _____.

   a. has come down with a cold from being in the rain

   b. is allergic to fruit

   c. has recently experienced the loss of a loved one

   d. is elderly

8. A person with a visual disability is someone who probably _____.

   a. needs a wheelchair

   b. can't hear well

   c. will die soon

   d. can't see well

9. A person who is allergic to nuts _____.

   a. eats nuts frequently

   b. can get sick if he or she eats nuts

   c. uses nuts often in cooking

   d. has never tasted nuts

10. One symptom of a potentially serious disease might be _____.

   a. being hungry for breakfast

   b. being in a happy mood

   c. losing weight quickly without dieting

   d. having lots of energy

H. Sense or Nonsense?

Using your knowledge of the unit's target vocabulary, write Y (yes) for statements that make sense or N (no) for statements that do not make sense.

1. _____ An injection might hurt when you get it, but it can also heal or prevent illness.

2. _____ Hot, inflamed, red skin is a common sign that a wound is healing.

3. _____ Frank was singing and smiling as he left the hospital. I think he was in a bad mood.

4. _____ An infected cut is healing properly.

5. _____ An incorrect diagnosis of cancer is not really a serious problem because it won't affect the treatment.

6. _____ Rats and cockroaches are a menace to society, partly because of the diseases that they can carry and spread.

7. _____ A sympathetic friend is one who understands your feelings.

8. _____ An outbreak of tuberculosis in our state resulted in 25 fatalities. Thankfully, no one died.

9. _____ World health officials have been surprised by the recurrence of polio. Until recently, they thought it was completely gone.

10. _____ When we talk about the mortality rate of infants, we are talking about how many babies are born alive and survive.

Unit 3

Sports

Word Form Chart

Noun	Verb	Adjective	Adverb
challenge challenger	**challenge**	challenging	
controversy		controversial	controversially
dedication	dedicate	**dedicated**	
energy	energize	energetic	energetically
fairness		**fair** unfair	fairly unfairly
ferocity		**fierce**	fiercely
glance	**glance**	glancing	
grip	**grip**	gripping	
horizon		**horizontal**	horizontally
intensity	intensify	**intense** intensive	intensely intensively
league			
persistence	**persist**	persistent	persistently
prominence		**prominent**	prominently
referee	referee		
reputation repute		reputed	reputedly
rival rivalry	rival	rival	
tournament			
whistle	whistle		

Definitions and Examples of Word Forms

1a. challenge, n., a difficult task

Sami felt he was up to the <u>challenge</u> of beating the university record for the annual marathon.

A triathlon, where you swim, cycle, and run in one day, is a <u>challenging</u> (adj.) event that is too difficult for many amateur athletes.

1b. challenge, v.t., to ask or dare someone to play a game or a sport; to test one's abilities

The swim team coach <u>challenged</u> each individual swimmer to improve her racing time by three seconds.

2. controversy, n., a serious disagreement about something that people have strong feelings about

There was a lot of <u>controversy</u> over whether the athlete who broke the rules should be allowed to continue to compete.

Many people argued over the Olympic Committee's <u>controversial</u> (adj.) decision to allow runners with artificial legs to compete in the 2012 London Olympics.

3. dedicated, adj., giving a lot of your energy and time to something

Tim is so <u>dedicated</u> to his amateur volleyball league that he often takes time off work to travel to matches.

Many parents <u>dedicate</u> (v.t.) all their spare time to coaching their children's sports teams, leaving them little time to stay physically fit themselves.

4. **energy,** n., power, liveliness, vitality

   Children with high <u>energy</u> benefit from participating in after-school sports.

   Some of the new protein drinks claim to <u>energize</u> (v.t.) you so that you can continue to be active even when you are tired.

5. **fair,** adj., with equal consideration for all, just, reasonable

   Boxing has specific rules that state what is and what is not a <u>fair</u> punch.

   In selecting judges for a sports competition, it is important to consider people who value <u>fairness</u> (n.) and who have a great deal of experience with the sport.

6. **fierce,** adj., powerful and strong

   The new rugby team faced <u>fierce</u> competition from older, more experienced teams in the league.

   Jonathan plays football with such <u>ferocity</u> (n.) that he sometimes injures players on the opposing team.

7. **glance,** v.i., to look very quickly at something and then look away

   We rushed into the stadium and <u>glanced</u> quickly at the scoreboard, only to see that our favorite football team, the Green Bay Packers, was losing.

   The figure skater stole a nervous <u>glance</u> (n.) at her coach after finishing her routine.

8. **grip,** v.t., to hold on to something tightly

   A U.S. football player wears special shoes that <u>grip</u> the field and help him run, even when it is slippery and wet.

   The famous golfer, Tiger Woods, tightened his <u>grip</u> (n.) on the golf club and concentrated before he started to swing.

9. **horizontal,** adj., flat, or level with the ground

   Runners in the Olympic hurdles race jump over 10 <u>horizontal</u> bars raised about one meter off the ground.

   The diver seemed to hang <u>horizontally</u> (adv.) in the air for a second before she shot straight down into the water.

10. **intense,** adj., extremely strong or serious

    Our high school principal feels that the level of competition in high school sports is too <u>intense</u> for young people, who feel pressure to win every time.

    The tennis coach watches all the matches very <u>intensely</u> (adv.) and refuses to be distracted by anything.

11. **league,** n., an association of sports teams that organizes matches for its member teams

    The Central Minnesota Women's Softball <u>League</u> has twelve teams from the region that compete during the summer months.

    My church minister wants members to form a team to compete in the newly formed local bowling <u>league</u>.

12. **persist,** v.i., to continue to do something, even when it is difficult or you are being told not to

    Rudy is a movie about Daniel "Rudy" Ruettiger, a young man who achieved his dream of playing on a college football team because he <u>persisted</u> in believing he could do it even when no one else did.

    Lukka was determined to get a spot on the swim team, and his hard work and <u>persistence</u> (n.) at tryouts paid off when he was chosen.

13. **prominent,** adj., well known and respected, important

    Geoff is a <u>prominent</u> track and field coach who is well known for his ability to inspire and encourage his runners.

    The field hockey team's state championship trophy was <u>prominently</u> (adv.) displayed in a glass case in the school's main lobby.

14. **referee,** n., the official at a game or sport who makes players follow the rules

    A soccer <u>referee</u> is responsible for starting and stopping the match, disciplining players, and generally making sure everyone follows the rules.

    My son Thomas enjoys earning a little extra money by <u>refereeing</u> (v.t.) matches for younger players in our local ice hockey league.

15. **reputation,** n., other people's opinions of a person's character and personality

    The internationally known Brazilian soccer player Pelé had a <u>reputation</u> for understanding and caring about the problems of the poor in his native country.

    The volleyball coach was of ill <u>repute</u> (n.) because he made a rude comment about the other team and was asked to leave the game.

16. **rival,** n., a person, team, or group that you have an ongoing competition with

    As one of the world's best soccer teams competing for the 2014 World Cup, Brazil's team beat one of its main <u>rivals</u>, the team from Mexico.

    England and Spain have a fierce <u>rivalry</u> (n.) in international soccer. Their fans are often ready to fight about who is best.

17. **tournament,** n., a series of matches or games played to determine a champion in a sport

    At the ice hockey <u>tournament</u> next weekend, eight different teams will play a series of games to decide the best team.

    Chess <u>tournaments</u> are popular among young players who are eager to compete.

18. **whistle,** n., a sharp, high-pitched musical noise; an instrument that makes this noise when someone blows it

    All the soccer players dropped to their knees after they heard the referee blow the <u>whistle</u> and realized that one of the players was hurt.

    When the softball coach saw that her players were not focusing on her instructions, she <u>whistled</u> (v.i.) loudly to get their attention.

Vocabulary Practice

A. Make the Connection

Choose the vocabulary word that is most closely related to each sentence.
The first one has been done as an example.

challenge	glanced	~~whistle~~
persisted	prominent	rivals
controversy	referee	gripped

1. The coach took the shiny metal object from around his neck and blew it
   to start the race. _____ **whistle** _____

2. I looked quickly at the opposing volleyball team captain to see if she
   looked worried about the match or not. _____

3. There was a lot of discussion but no agreement about the school board's
   decision to kick the star basketball player off the team for cheating.

   _____

4. Tom was determined to improve his batting average, so he kept
   practicing even during the winter. _____

5. Anne is a very well-known table tennis player who is respected for her
   technique and skill. _____

6. Someone has to be in charge of athletic competitions to start and stop
   them and to make sure that the players behave and follow the rules.

   _____

7. To run 26 miles in a marathon is a difficult task for most people.

   _____

8. McGee High and Central High are the two best football teams in
   the city, and they always compete for the championship.

   _____

9. The young golfer held her club too tightly because she was nervous about
   playing in her first tournament. _____

B. What's the Word?

With your partner, fill in each box on the grid. Student A will use Grid A. Student B will use Grid B in Appendix 1 on page 166. Each grid is missing different words. Describe the words on your grid so your partner can fill in his or her blank spaces. When all of the blanks are full, compare your grids to see if you have the correct answers.

> **Example:** For Box 1, Student A could give Student B these clues: *It's an adverb; powerfully; with great concentration. You practice like this when you're getting ready for a big game.*

Grid A

1 intensely	5	9 rival	13
2	6	10 gripped	14
3 challenge	7 fiercely	11	15 controversy
4	8 persist	12 fairness	16

C. Off Base

The underlined word in each sentence does not make sense. Cross out each underlined word or phrase, and replace it with a vocabulary word from the unit that fits the context. The first one has been done as an example.

1. Jake approached his workouts with a/an ~~laziness~~ *intensity*   and a concentration that surprised even himself.

2. The swim coach told Marlee to imagine herself slicing through the water underline{straight up and down}_____ as she swam.

3. Leo underline{released}_____ the bat hard and prayed that he would hit a home run.

4. Jessica hopes to defeat her long-time underline{teammate}_____ at the next track and field meet.

5. The athletic sportswear company was happy that the underline{little known}_____ Native American athlete Billy Mills agreed to advertise its new line of running shoes.

6. The Senior Olympics are for people over the age of 50 who want to face the underline{easy task}_____ of staying in shape and competing as they get older.

7. The ice hockey referee was disliked by many people because of a
   popular _____ decision he made to end the game early
   after a fight broke out in the stands.

8. Sherri <u>stared</u> _____ at the TV cameras briefly before
   settling down to swing her golf club.

D. In the Wrong Place

In each paragraph, the underlined vocabulary words are in the wrong place. Cross out the inappropriate word and replace it with the underlined word that makes sense. The first one has been done as an example.

1. Jackie and Lyla were best friends. They enjoyed the friendly competition of playing baseball together. They were both gifted and ~~tournament~~ *dedicated* athletes. They won their first ~~rivals~~ *tournament* and celebrated together. However, after a huge fight when they were sixteen, Jackie and Lyla became fierce ~~dedicated~~ *rivals*.

2. One of the important things about playing tennis is the intensity_____ the player has on the racket. The grip_____ can often interpret the other player's emotions and glancing_____ by challenger_____ at how she holds it.

3. Fiercely_____ play is an interesting concept that is central to team sports. The difference between playing whistle_____ and cheating can sometimes be hard to define. If the score is tied, when the fair_____ blows his or her controversy_____ to call a penalty on a player, it may create a referee_____.

4. In order to succeed in sports as well as in life, you must have good values. <u>Fairness</u> is a characteristic that will help you to keep working hard even when things are not going well. Furthermore, <u>persistence</u> at school, work, or on a team is necessary for success. In addition, <u>dedication</u> is a value that is promoted by both civil and religious institutions so that society works well for everyone.

5. Unfortunately, sometimes the parents of children who play sports do not behave very well. Our local soccer <u>challenge</u> faces a serious <u>intensely</u> because so many parents compete <u>energy</u> even though they are not on the field. I wish they would just put their <u>league</u> into something more positive than yelling insults at little children who come to play and have a good time.

Frequent Collocations: Sports

Some common sports collocations are listed. What others can you think of?

1. **challenge**—biggest/greatest challenge, to be up to the challenge, to face/meet a challenge, a major challenge
2. **controversy**—a controversial issue/decision, a controversy over something, to generate controversy
3. **fair**—to be fair to say, fair play, one's fair share
4. **fierce**—a fierce battle, a fierce competition, to be fiercely competitive
5. **glance**—at a glance, at first glance, a quick glance, to shoot a glance
6. **grip**—to get/have a grip on, to have a firm grip on, to lose one's grip on
7. **intense**—high intensity, intense competition, intense pressure
8. **prominent**—to be a prominent member of, prominent leaders, a prominent role
9. **reputation**—to develop a reputation as, to earn/gain a reputation for
10. **rival**—to be bitter rivals, a chief rival, a rivalry between X and Y

E. Balancing Act

Using the list of frequent collocations, fill in the missing words in the columns to form collocations. The first one has been done as an example.

Column A	Column B
1. *controversial*	issue
2. lose one's	_____
3. _____	play
4. a chief	_____
5. high	_____
6. _____	a challenge
7. _____	role
8. quick	_____
9. _____	competitive
10. gain	_____

F. Get It Together

Unscramble the words and phrases to write sentences containing the collocations. The first one has been done as an example.

1. to play their best / meeting / Anna and Jen / always enjoyed / the challenge

   Anna and Jen always enjoyed meeting the challenge to

   play their best.

2. grip on the ball / Andy keeps / he's bowling / a firm / When

   _____

   _____

3. the team / because / are nervous / The parents / faces a major / this weekend / challenge

   _____

   _____

4. over / The coach / the final score / about the controversy / was disappointed

   _____

   _____

5. a soccer player / is determined to be / Rhiannon / pressure / the intense / in spite of / of tryouts

_____

_____

6. play / Coach Jones / the rules of / all the players / fair / asked / to follow

_____

_____

7. There is / fierce / from the other runners / in the state tournament / competition

_____

_____

8. understood / Evanston's star quarterback / glance / after a / the other team's strategy / quick / at the field

_____

_____

Practice Quiz

G. The Choice Is Yours

Circle the best answer.

1. If your sail is horizontal, your boat _____.

    a. is straight up and down

    b. is going fast

    c. is in danger of sinking

    d. makes for an easy ride

2. When there is controversy surrounding the use of steroids among Olympic athletes, the media usually _____.

    a. doesn't present anything new

    b. is not sure what it is about

    c. presents the arguments on both sides

    d. presents one side only

3. A prominent athlete is _____.

    a. tall

    b. well known

    c. shy

    d. retired

4. Dedicated sports fans might _____.

    a. know all possible facts about each member of their favorite team

    b. prefer listening to music over watching sports

    c. attend games mostly for the company of their friends

    d. not understand the rules of the game

5. If you glance at the rule book for tennis, you _____.

    a. study it carefully

    b. look at it quickly

    c. memorize it

    d. copy it

6. Two athletes who are rivals will probably be _____.

    a. unhappy

    b. understanding

    c. emotional

    d. competitive

7. Sam was gripping the baseball bat incorrectly, so he was _____.

    a. rolling it wrong

    b. choosing it wrong

    c. holding it wrong

    d. throwing it wrong

8. At exactly 8:00 AM, the marathon race official blew his whistle, so _____.

     a. the runners all began the race

     b. the snack carts started selling sandwiches

     c. the people watching started talking

     d. the runners stopped

9. When your team is a member of a local softball league, it _____.

     a. plays in a different country every week

     b. has coffee together after the game

     c. competes against other member teams

     d. receives a medal for being the best

10. If a runner does laps around the track energetically, she might run _____.

     a. slowly

     b. without making an effort

     c. at a steady pace

     d. quickly

H. Sense or Nonsense?

Using your knowledge of the unit's target vocabulary, write Y (yes) for statements that make sense or N (no) for statements that do not make sense.

1. _____ The professional basketball team was eliminated from the tournament because the players used illegal drugs.

2. _____ Everyone in the community of Highmore agreed with the school board's highly controversial decision to support the successful women's field hockey team.

3. _____ Victor has persistent ankle pain that affects his ability to run. It's a condition that he can't seem to cure.

4. _____ Marc didn't get nervous before a match because he felt intense pressure to compete and do well.

5. _____ If the coaches or players disagree with a referee's decision, arguing with her will not help because she makes the final decision.

6. _____ The upcoming match with Carleton, whose players were all smaller and inexperienced, posed a challenge to the Macalester rugby team.

7. _____ Sydney is reputed to be an excellent coach because of his patience and his ability to push the players to excel.

8. _____ The fierce competition among countries who want to host the FIFA World Cup tournament means that the committee has several options to choose from.

9. _____ If a football coach treats his players unfairly, they will be sure to play their hardest for him.

10. _____ Snowboarders whose nervous energy is too high may fail on the jumps.

Unit 4

Transportation

Word Form Chart

Noun	Verb	Adjective	Adverb
abandonment	**abandon**	abandoned	
access accessibility	access	access accessible	accessibly
anticipation	**anticipate**	anticipated	
circumstances		circumstantial	circumstantially
		crucial	crucially
entitlement	**entitle**	entitled	
fare			
gear	gear		
impact	impact		
interruption	**interrupt**	interrupted	
mobility	mobilize	**mobile** immobile	
parallel	parallel	**parallel**	
peak	peak	peak	
pilot	pilot	piloted	
situation	situate	situated	
		steep	steeply
	undergo		
	urbanize	**urban** suburban	

Definitions and Examples of Word Forms

1. **abandon,** v.t., to leave someone or something that you are responsible for

    Juan <u>abandoned</u> the car at the side of the road because it didn't work.

    There are very few <u>abandoned</u> (adj.) cars in Oakville because many police officers patrol there.

2. **access,** n., the way into a place; the ability to get at something

    <u>Access</u> to Exit 10 is restricted because of a flood.

    The Lees live in the country, and the house is <u>accessible</u> (adj.) only by a dirt road.

3. **anticipate,** v.t., to know that something is going to happen and to be prepared for it

    When driving, try to <u>anticipate</u> what the other drivers will do so you won't be surprised.

    Some passengers feel a sense of <u>anticipation</u> (n.) when the plane is about to land.

4. **circumstances,** n., (usually plural), facts or events in a particular situation

    When there is a railroad accident, the police need to investigate the <u>circumstances</u> that led to it.

    The <u>circumstances</u> surrounding the loss of the shipment of Chilean fruit are not clear.

5. **crucial,** adj., extremely necessary

Listening to the air traffic controller is <u>crucial</u> for airline pilots, especially at large airports where there is a lot of traffic.

Whether to take the 217 bus or the 218 bus is not a <u>crucially</u> (adv.) important decision. They both go downtown.

6. **entitle,** v.t., to give someone the right to something

In most countries, the law <u>entitles</u> you to file a lawsuit if you are hit by a drunk driver.

Just because James knew the police chief, it didn't mean he was <u>entitled</u> to ignore the law.

7. **fare,** n., the amount you pay to travel by bus, taxi, plane, or train

Do you have change? I have to pay my bus <u>fare</u>.

The train <u>fare</u> to Philadelphia is actually more expensive than I expected.

8. **gear,** n., a wheel used to transfer power from one part of a machine to another

I'm stuck because my bike's <u>gears</u> slipped and the chain fell off.

Car motors use less gasoline if you put them in the highest <u>gear</u> possible.

9. **impact,** n., the force of one thing hitting another; having an effect on something

In Highland Park, a car drove off the road last night and hit a restaurant near the road. The <u>impact</u> of the wreck left a huge hole in the wall.

The news of General Vallejo's death in a plane crash had a huge <u>impact</u> on the people of his country.

10. **interrupt,** v.t., to stop someone or something from saying or doing something, often for a short period of time

    It is not a good idea to <u>interrupt</u> a police officer when he or she is giving you a ticket!

    The <u>interruption</u> (n.) in the flow of traffic was caused by a train as it passed through Valparaiso, Indiana.

11. **mobile,** adj., able to move or be moved

    A <u>mobile</u> phone is useful when you are traveling. Your GPS app helps you find your destination quickly and easily.

    Americans in general value <u>mobility</u> (n.); many like to travel to other cities.

12. **parallel,** adj., two things that keep the same distance between them for their entire length; parking on the street along the curb

    <u>Parallel</u> parking was the most difficult part of the driver's license exam for Brenda. She almost didn't pass!

    If Henry wants to get to the truck stop to eat lunch, he should turn left after the bridge. The restaurant's parking lot <u>parallels</u> (v.t.) the river.

13. **peak,** n., the highest point or level

    The mountain's <u>peak</u> is about five miles up the road. After that, the road is all downhill.

    Charles hates the <u>peak</u> (adj.) traffic hour, or rush hour, when everyone returns home from work.

14. **pilot,** n., person who flies an aircraft or steers a ship

    The <u>pilot</u> landed the plane in a cornfield because she was out of fuel.

    Ahmed is <u>piloting</u> (v.t.) the boat because he knows the shortest route.

15. **situation,** n., events and conditions that exist at a particular moment; location

    After arriving at the scene of the crime, the detectives radioed the <u>situation</u> to police headquarters.

    The Holiday Hotel parking lot is <u>situated</u> (v.t.) on the hill behind the mall.

16. **steep,** adj., at a sharp upward angle

    The road up the mountain is <u>steep</u> and dangerous, so Ning took the longer route that goes through the valley.

    The price of gasoline has increased <u>steeply</u> (adv.) recently.

17. **undergo,** v.t., to have a change happen, sometimes a negative experience

    Henrietta Chen had to <u>undergo</u> 12 hours of surgery after the near-fatal accident when the bridge collapsed.

    Pilots <u>undergo</u> many hours of intense training before they can fly.

18. **urban,** adj., having to do with a city

    The <u>urban</u> area is difficult to drive in because of population increase.

    The Phillips family used to live in the country, but now their area has been <u>urbanized</u> (v.) so they are closer to restaurants and gas stations.

Vocabulary Practice

A. Make the Connection

Choose the vocabulary word that is most closely related to each sentence.
The first one has been done as an example.

circumstances	peak	fare
gear	anticipate	undergo
abandoned	accessible	~~parallel~~

1. The parking test is so difficult because you must park along the edge of the street without hitting the curb. _____**parallel**_____

2. The police officer filled out a report on what happened when Jacob ran into the cyclist. _____

3. When the roads are icy, you must think ahead about how you are going to stop. _____

4. John had to take a blood test because the police officer thought he might be driving under the influence of alcohol (D.U.I.). _____

5. You can shift your bicycle to make it easier to pedal when riding at different speeds. _____

6. The heaviest traffic hours are made worse when people slow down to go through tunnels or because of accidents. _____

7. Amir would save money if he took the bus because the bus costs far less than parking. _____

8. Thieves will often leave stolen cars in remote locations. _____

9. It is difficult to get to the remote ski lodge when the mountain roads are icy. _____

B. Branching Out

Write the correct form of the word. Refer to the Word Form Chart if necessary. You may have to change the verb form. The first one has been done as an example.

1. **impact**

   a. The _____ *impact* _____ of the train going off the track was felt for miles.

   b. When something _____ a vehicle, the airbags will inflate.

   c. The clearest sign of the _____ of the transportation strike was the number of people who had to walk to work.

2. **pilot**

   a. The ship was _____ by an expert. It returned safely to the harbor after the storm.

   b. The automatic _____ system on the ship stopped working, so the ship had to be guided back home manually.

   c. They are going to give the _____ a hero's welcome for landing the plane safely in the Hudson River.

3. **access**

   a. Do not go into that office! _____ is limited to supervisors.

   b. You can _____ the City Office of Traffic Control online.

   c. Jane Connelly is the mayor. If you are angry, send her an email about the _____ of parking downtown.

4. **mobile**

   a. Johanna's truck is not _____ because of the huge winter storm this weekend. It is stuck under three feet of snow.

   b. The traffic report says that _____ on the highway is limited due to ice and snow.

   c. If Johanna and others get stuck, the mayor will have to _____ city resources to get them out.

5. **interrupt**

   a. Gary got a flat tire on his way home, which threatened to _____ his plans to visit Jan.

   b. When he tried to contact Jan, the call did not go through. Something _____ the cell phone signal.

   c. When Gary finally did get to speak with her, it was hard to hear her because of the continued _____ in the signal.

6. **urban**

   a. Gene knows that driving his car to work and shopping every day is bad for the environment, but he loves living in his big, grassy _____ neighborhood.

   b. If Gene lived in a/an _____ area, he could walk to work or take public transportation.

   c. However, cities are not all good. The push to _____ means more people have to use the same resources.

C. Off Base

The underlined word in each sentence does not make sense. Cross out each underlined word or phrase, and replace it with a vocabulary word from the unit that fits the context. The first one has been done as an example.

1. The results of Shin's driving test were ~~unexpected~~ *anticipated*. He thought he would pass and he did.

2. Don't walk close to the edge of that road up to the mountain valley_____ because there is no railing to prevent you from falling.

3. Mohammad thought that the climb on his bicycle was difficult because the hill was so flat_____.

4. If you like to do lots of cultural activities without having to drive very far, move to a more <u>rural</u>   area.

5. I like to be very <u>stationary</u>   because travel is exciting and interesting.

6. Adams Street and Main Street are <u>perpendicular</u>   . You can't get to Main from Adams because they do not intersect.

7. Details in the robbery are <u>unimportant</u>   . The police need all the information they can get to help find the person who robbed the train.

8. The entry to the park is <u>open</u>   to cars, trucks, and motorcycles.

9. Working in the public transportation office does not <u>allow</u>   Anya to a free bus pass.

D. What's Missing?

Fill in the blanks in the paragraph with a word from the list that fits the context. The first one has been done as an example.

peak	access	interruption
mobility	parallel	impact
~~crucial~~	urban	undergoing

City traffic planners have a tough job. When planning transportation patterns, they must keep many things in mind. First, it is _____*crucial*_____ to consider the way that the main streets are used by drivers. For example, there may be little or no _____ to them at times due to the number of drivers on the road. It may be wise for motorists not to try to enter these streets and to try alternate routes. Another important thing to keep in mind is the flow of cars and trucks on the streets. During _____ hours, traffic jams are common. It can be especially slow getting to work in the morning because of limited _____. Third, there is a potential for traffic accidents if things are poorly planned. Important routes that are _____ repairs can create traffic jams that last for hours. Finally, sometimes accidents happen when the road is not well taken care of and holes form. The _____ on the traffic can be serious in those cases. In fact, planning city traffic patterns is a complex and important job.

Frequent Collocations: Transportation

Some common transportation collocations are listed. What others can you think of?

1. **access**—direct access to, easy access to, free access to
2. **circumstances**—ordinary circumstances, similar circumstances, under no/any/such circumstances
3. **crucial**—crucial moment, to ask a crucial question, to play a crucial role in
4. **gear**—a gear shift, high/low gear, to put/get into gear
5. **mobile**—a mobile home, a mobile phone, a mobile unit
6. **parallel**—a parallel line, to run in a parallel direction, to run parallel to
7. **peak**—highest peak, a mountain peak, a peak period
8. **pilot**—a pilot program, a plane/boat/helicopter pilot, a test pilot, to be on/run on automatic pilot
9. **situation**—a desperate/dangerous situation, the present situation, a serious/critical situation
10. **steep**—a steep climb, steep hill/mountain, a steep slope/incline

E. Not Meant To Be

These collocations are incorrect. Read all of the underlined words, and choose the one that best matches or collocates with the first word. Use the list of frequent collocations to help you. The first one has been done as an example.

1. ~~easy~~ peak   *easy access* _____

2. mountain <u>pilot</u>   _____

3. test <u>~~access~~</u>   _____

4. steep <u>gear</u>   _____

5. dangerous <u>home</u>   _____

6. run <u>slope</u>   _____

7. high <u>situation</u>   _____

8. mobile <u>parallel to</u> _____

___

F. Get It Together

Unscramble the words and phrases to write sentences containing the collocations. The first one has been done as an example.

1. the steering wheel / The gear / is located / shift / next to

    <u>The gear shift is located next to the steering wheel.</u>

2. Travel / a crucial / plays / of the United States / in the economy / role

    _____

    _____

3. peak / when travelling / Slow down / over the mountain

    _____

    _____

4. is easy / the driving test / circumstances / Passing / under / ordinary

    _____

    _____

5. home / Jan and Lindsey / in their mobile / went to Nicaragua

_____

_____

6. cars / One day / pilot / able to run on / automatic / may be

_____

_____

7. Route 80 / Route 90 / parallel to / runs

_____

_____

8. There is / situation / a dangerous / an accident / because of / in that intersection

_____

_____

Practice Quiz

G. The Choice Is Yours

Circle the best answer.

1. An area could be urban if it has _____.

   a. no public transportation

   b. on-street parking meters

   c. tractors and horses

   d. mostly cars and trucks

2. If you have to undergo surgery as a result of a car accident, it is probably _____.

   a. a lot of fun

   b. easy to access

   c. fairly common

   d. a critical situation

3. If a television news story about rising fuel prices makes a big impact on you, you would be likely to _____.

   a. tell many people about it

   b. forget that you heard it

   c. mention it in passing

   d. ignore it

4. If Chen is mobile, he can _____.

    a. easily move from place to place

    b. stay at home tonight

    c. move with the help of a helicopter

    d. carry a phone in his pocket

5. A ship's pilot must behave cautiously when _____.

    a. the weather is good

    b. there are no other ships in sight

    c. the ship is entering a busy port

    d. the captain is having a party

6. You will have to pay a fare if you _____.

    a. are a truck driver

    b. own your own boat

    c. drive your own car

    d. take a public bus

7. Traffic flow might be interrupted by _____.

    a. a butterfly flying low

    b. a little rain

    c. a forest beside the road

    d. a tree across the road

8. When Vitaly's hot-air balloon landed on the peak of a hill, he _____.

    a. could see the whole valley below him

    b. was sitting in a flat field

    c. had landed near a riverbank

    d. was halfway down the hill

9. After Jin's accident with the taxi, the insurance company wanted _____.

    a. to know only the main circumstances

    b. to hear all the circumstances

    c. to hear mostly Jin's circumstances

    d. to learn about the taxi driver's circumstances

10. It is crucial for drivers of private cars to _____.

    a. have a commercial driver's license

    b. talk on the cell phone while driving

    c. watch out for traffic signals and signs

    d. ignore traffic police

H. Sense or Nonsense?

Using your knowledge of the unit's target vocabulary, write Y (yes) for statements that make sense or N (no) for statements that do not make sense.

1. _____ The abandoned bicycle Ian found in the park was broken.

2. _____ In Kenji's neighborhood, there is no signal for his cell phone, which means that the signal is accessible from his house.

3. _____ Sheila was packing her bags in anticipation of her next vacation.

4. _____ When a vehicle is stolen, witnesses often have information that is crucial to recovering it.

5. _____ If your car is damaged in an accident, you may be entitled to receive money from the insurance company of the person who hit you so that you can repair your car.

6. _____ Gregory likes to drive on wide roads with little traffic. He should try the urban area.

7. _____ Sarah's car would not go into gear, so she couldn't drive home.

8. _____ It is a good situation for business when a country has many types of transportation available.

9. _____ Parallel to the curb about three feet away is a good rule to follow when you park your car.

10. _____ Jeremy likes steep roads because it is easy to drive his large truck on them.

Fashion and Design

Word Form Chart

Noun	Verb	Adjective	Adverb
contemporary		**contemporary**	contemporarily
fascination	**fascinate**	fascinated fascinating	fascinatingly
flaw		flawed	
glow	**glow**	glowing	glowingly
medium/media		**medium**	
paleness	pale	**pale**	palely
precedent	**precede**	preceding unprecedented	
restriction	**restrict**	restricted restrictive	
ridicule	ridicule	**ridiculous**	ridiculously
rip	**rip**	ripped	
stain	**stain**	stained	
symmetry		**symmetrical**	symmetrically
synthetic	synthesize	**synthetic**	synthetically
transparency		**transparent**	transparently
ultimate		**ultimate**	ultimately
versatility		**versatile**	versatilely
vividness		**vivid**	vividly

Definitions and Examples

1a. **contemporary**, adj., something that exists or is happening now; modern

Mariela doesn't like to buy old or used clothes; she likes more <u>contemporary</u> styles from current designers.

1b. **contemporary**, n., someone or something that exists at the same time as someone or something else

Christian Dior was a <u>contemporary</u> of Coco Chanel, who designed popular clothing during the 1950s.

2. **fascinate**, v.t., to cause strong interest or to attract a lot of attention

Every year during New York City's fashion week, the designers' collections <u>fascinate</u> editors from major magazines.

Susana's blouse <u>fascinated</u> everyone at the party because it was made of feathers and leather.

4. **flaw**, n., something wrong, or a mistake, that causes something not to be perfect

The wedding gown was perfect except for one small <u>flaw</u>: a missing button on the sleeve.

Jack bought a <u>flawed</u> (adj.) pair of jeans at an outlet store for less than half of the price of a perfect pair.

5. **glow,** v.i., to shine with soft light

The photographer used soft lighting to make the model's skin <u>glow</u>.

Henri's diamond watch has a blue light that <u>glows</u> and helps him see the time in the dark.

6a. **medium,** adj., a size or amount that is not big but not small

Ana likes to wear a <u>medium</u> heel on her shoes. If the heels are flat, she feels too short, but if they're too high, she has trouble walking in them.

6b. **medium,** n., a way of distributing information, usually in the plural (media)

Many large companies use magazine and television ads as the <u>media</u> for advertising their fashions because readers want to know where they can buy the new looks.

7. **pale,** adj., with very little color or without strong color

The designer wanted the models to look <u>pale</u>, so the make-up artist used very little color on the model's cheeks.

The <u>paleness</u> (n.) of Cari's blue boots made them look almost white.

8. **precede,** v.t., to come before something or someone

When fashion designers have an idea for a new suit, they first draw pictures of the idea; these drawings <u>precede</u> the production of the clothing.

The first bikini was made in 1945, and it was the <u>precedent</u> (n.) for all of the tiny bathing suits on beaches today.

9. **restrict,** v.t., to limit what someone or something can do

   We wanted to go to the designer's party after the runway show, but the host <u>restricted</u> the entry to guests named on a special list.

   After Joel spent $3,000 on a new wardrobe last week, his mother <u>restricted</u> his credit card purchases to $500 each month.

10. **ridiculous,** adj., something foolish or unreasonable

    It was <u>ridiculous</u> for Lucy to wear her high heels on ice because she could not walk in them and fell down twice.

    Ivan <u>ridiculed</u> (v.t.) Megan because she spent $10,000 on a new handbag even though she couldn't pay her rent.

11. **rip,** v.t., v.i., to tear something; to pull something apart

    Grace's shirt <u>ripped</u> when she pulled it over her head, creating a big hole.

    Saeed has a <u>rip</u> (n.) in his sweater where he caught his ring on the thread and pulled it apart.

12. **stain,** v.t., v.i., to leave a mark on something that is difficult or impossible to remove

    Gavin spilled his coffee and <u>stained</u> his girlfriend's white jacket.

    Benicio's favorite sweatshirt was covered with grass and dirt <u>stains</u> (n.) from playing soccer, so his wife threw it away.

13. **symmetrical,** adj., having identical or balanced halves, or sides, when viewed from the front

    Studies have shown that many fashion models are considered beautiful because their faces are perfectly <u>symmetrical</u>; the left side is exactly the same as the right side.

    Min loves when his outfits have <u>symmetry</u> (n.), so he bought a new jacket that has two identical pockets on each side.

14. **synthetic,** adj., not natural, made of human-made materials

    Aasif doesn't buy <u>synthetic</u> shirts because he thinks that natural materials feel better against his skin.

    The <u>synthetic</u> material that is used to make Victoria's socks is produced by combining chemicals.

15. **transparent,** adj., something that can be seen through

    Lili has a raincoat that is <u>transparent</u>, so even when it's raining, you can still see her outfit.

    I don't like the <u>transparency</u> (n.) of this fabric for a dress to be worn in public.

16. **ultimate,** adj., the most important, or strongest, example of something; in the end; after everything else has been done

    Some people consider fur coats to be the <u>ultimate</u> symbol of wealth because you cannot buy one if you don't have a lot of money.

    Krista tries to wear very short skirts to school, but her mother always makes the <u>ultimate</u> decision about her outfits. She makes Krista change into a longer skirt every morning.

17. **versatile,** adj., able to do many things, or able to be used for many purposes

    This dress is <u>versatile</u>, so I can wear it with flat shoes for work or with high heels for a dinner party.

    Jon likes the <u>versatility</u> (n.) of his coat. He can leave the lining in for colder days, or he can remove the lining for warmer weather.

18. **vivid,** adj., very clear and strong

    Aisha gave us a <u>vivid</u> description of her wedding dress. She was very excited and told us about every detail.

    Most of the women at the concert were wearing black dresses, so the <u>vivid</u> color of Jo's red outfit was really noticeable.

Vocabulary Practice

A. Match Point

Write the letter of the best example next to each word. The first one has been done as an example.

1. __c__   glowing   a. a giant pink hat on a grandmother

2. ____   ridiculous   b. spilling coffee on your nightgown

3. ____   stain   ~~c.~~ the model's makeup

4. ____   rip   d. red dress and shoes

5. ____   vivid   e. getting your coat caught on a nail

6. ____   precedes   f. putting on socks before shoes

7. ____   fascinating   g. a skirt missing a button hole

8. ____   flaw   h. a famous model's lifestyle

9. ____   versatile   i. a dark-colored cardigan

10. ____   ultimate   j. gym shorts at a fancy restaurant

B. In the Wrong Place

In each paragraph, the underlined vocabulary words are in the wrong place. Cross out the inappropriate word and replace it with the underlined word that makes sense. The first one has been done as an example.

1. Katie's dad wears the same pair of sweatpants every weekend. They used to be a bright red color, but they have been washed so many times that now they are ~~ripped~~ *pale* pink. They have grass ~~ultimate~~ *stains* all over them, and they are ~~pale~~ *ripped* from when he works in the yard. He says they are the ~~stains~~ *ultimate* in comfort.

2. In today's society, many people are flaws _____ by movie stars. Several glow _____ magazines and television shows describe the fashions that actors and actresses wear. In the news, these stars can seem to have no ultimately _____. They just contemporary _____ in their beautiful designer clothing. Sometimes people try to copy the outfits of the rich and famous, but fascinated _____, it is very difficult to buy this kind of look at prices everyone can afford.

3. Robert always likes his little dog Clyde to look fashionable. Robert bought Clyde a beautiful purple ridiculous _____ leather leash. He is not very good at versatile _____ Clyde with it, though, and Clyde always trots down the street in front. So Robert ordered a matching purple bag that is really synthetic _____; when he is not carrying Clyde in the bag, he can unzip it to use as a dog bed. Robert also dresses Clyde in a purple sweater when they go out. Some people laugh and think that Clyde looks restricting _____, but Robert thinks he's the most stylish dog in the neighborhood.

C. What's the Word?

With your partner, fill in each box on the grid. Student A will use Grid A. Student B will use Grid B in Appendix 1 on page 167. Each grid is missing different words. Describe the words on your grid so your partner can fill in his or her blank spaces. When all of the blanks are full, compare your grids to see if you have the correct answers.

> **Example:** For Box 1, Student A could give Student B these clues: *It's an adjective; clear and strong. It's a bright color; easy to see.*

Grid A

1 vivid	5	9 fascinate	13 rip
2	6 ridicule	10 precede	14
3	7 stain	11	15
4 flaw	8	12	16 glow

D. Off Base

The underlined word in each sentence does not make sense. Cross out each underlined word or phrase, and replace it with a vocabulary word from the unit that fits the context. The first one has been done as an example.

1. Pia likes a lot of attention, so she usually wears ~~neutral~~ *vivid* colors.

2. Cameron wore a shirt under his sweater because the sweater was so thin that it was <u>impossible to see through</u> _____.

3. Billie selects clothing made of <u>natural</u> _____ materials because man-made fabrics are easy to wash and last a long time.

4. Sometimes the weather <u>gives us freedom with</u> _____ our fashion choices. For example, it's usually not a good idea to wear your favorite shorts in the middle of winter.

5. Larry's appearance was <u>perfect</u> _____ because he had an ink stain on his tie.

6. Len is always the first in line to buy the newest clothing from his favorite designer. He would never wear anything that isn't <u>old and out of date</u> _____.

7. Jack shines his father's gold watch so carefully every day that it <u>has a dull, dark appearance</u> _____.

Frequent Collocations: Fashion and Design

Some common fashion and design collocations are listed. What others can you think of?

1. **contemporary**—contemporary art, contemporary design, to be a contemporary of
2. **flaw**—to be without flaw, to find flaw with, a fatal flaw
3. **glow**—a warm glow, glowing cheeks, to have a soft glow
4. **media**—media attention, media coverage, mass media
5. **pale**—pale eyes, pale blue/green/yellow/color, to pale in comparison
6. **ridiculous**—to seem/appear ridiculous, to be simply ridiculous, to be the object of ridicule
7. **stain**—a red/dark stain, a stain remover, to be stain-resistant
8. **synthetic**—synthetic dyes, synthetic fiber/material
9. **ultimate**—ultimate effect, ultimate goal/purpose, to be the ultimate
10. **vivid**—to have a vivid imagination, to paint a vivid picture of, vivid green/blue/colors

E. Balancing Act

Using the list of frequent collocations, fill in the missing words in the columns to form collocations. The first one has been done as an example.

Column A	Column B
1. <u>contemporary</u>	art
2. _____	dyes
3. _____	flaw
4. ultimate	_____
5. warm	_____
6. _____	imagination
7. _____	media
8. stain	_____
9. simply	_____
10. _____	eyes

F. Complete the Thought

Fill in the blank in each collocation with a unit vocabulary word. The first one has been done as an example.

1. Her mother found a _____*flaw*_____ with the wedding dress, but the bride was so beautiful that no one else noticed.

2. That skirt is not appropriate for a formal party because it has a dark _____ on it.

3. Leah likes to go outside in winter because cold weather gives her _____ cheeks.

4. Babies in the United States are traditionally dressed in _____ blue or pink.

5. _____ design is clean and modern.

6. Some people prefer natural fabrics to _____ materials.

7. Don't wear your city fashions in the country or you might appear _____.

Practice Quiz

G. The Choice Is Yours

Circle the best answer.

1. Zach was pale and tired at his sister's birthday party because _____.

   a. he worked all night finishing his sister's birthday dress

   b. he went to bed early

   c. he was afraid of a fire

   d. he had a sunburn

2. If your skirt is the ultimate example of a miniskirt, it is _____.

   a. really ugly

   b. really warm

   c. the best miniskirt ever made

   d. the most expensive miniskirt ever made

3. Vlad's wallet is completely transparent, so you can _____.

   a. open it easily

   b. put a lot of money into it

   c. clean it easily

   d. see through it

4. Molly's vivid dress ____.

   a. is all brown

   b. is white with small pink flowers

   c. is black and gray

   d. is bright red and orange

5. An absolutely fascinating fashion show is ____.

   a. extremely interesting and special

   b. really boring

   c. five hours long

   d. held outside

6. A versatile scarf ____.

   a. matches only one coat

   b. is only needed in the winter

   c. can also be used as a belt

   d. feels nice around your neck

7. Synthetic pants are made of ____.

   a. natural fabrics

   b. expensive fabrics

   c. machine-made fabrics

   d. soft fabrics

8. Gary's new shirt is flawed because it _____.

    a. is completely perfect

    b. has a button missing

    c. is his favorite shirt

    d. has two pockets

9. All of Magda's jewelry is contemporary. It was made _____.

    a. in the 1940s

    b. in a foreign country

    c. recently

    d. by her great-grandfather

10. A warm glow in a store's dressing room will probably _____.

    a. make the clothes look too large

    b. show all the features of the clothes

    c. hide flaws so you look better in the clothes

    d. make you look thinner

H. Sense or Nonsense?

Using your knowledge of the unit's target vocabulary, write Y (yes) for statements that make sense or N (no) for statements that do not make sense.

1. _____ Jason's suit coat has one pocket in the same place on each side. His coat is perfectly symmetrical.

2. _____ Keisha could not stop staring at Omar's gold rings. Keisha was not at all fascinated by his jewelry.

3. _____ If you look in Adam's closet, all you will see is white, black, or brown clothing. Adam loves vivid colors.

4. _____ Sue laughs at Ivan every time he wears a striped shirt with checked pants. Sue thinks that this combination looks ridiculous.

5. _____ Every Friday, Marcel goes to get a haircut, and then he shops for a new t-shirt. Marcel's shopping always precedes his haircuts.

6. _____ Tim always wears a tie that has his school colors on it because he likes contemporary design.

7. _____ Carey spilled juice all over her favorite jeans, but she still wears them because she doesn't mind having some stains on dark clothing.

8. _____ When Aimee buys a new top, she always buys a size small, but it is always too tight on her. She would probably be more comfortable in a size medium.

9. _____ Safety pins can be used to hold ripped clothing together.

10. _____ Joy can't wear sandals to work in the summer because the company safety policy restricts the type of shoes that can be worn.

Food and Nutrition

Word Form Chart

Noun	Verb	Adjective	Adverb
		adequate	adequately
		apparent	**apparently**
assembly	**assemble**	assembled	
calorie		caloric	
capacity			
disgust	**disgust**	disgusting disgusted	disgustedly
distinction		**distinct** distinctive	distinctly
flexibility		**flexible**	flexibly
ingredient			
means			
nutrition nutritionist		**nutritious** nutritional	nutritionally
portion	portion		
range	range		
		raw	
recipe			
regard	**regard**	regardless	
reversal reverse	**reverse**	reversible reverse	
starvation	**starve**	starved starving	

Definitions and Examples of Word Forms

1. **adequate,** adj., enough; as much as you need

    Our food budget didn't seem <u>adequate</u> for a family of four, but after we cut out soda and junk food, we had enough money.

    This old tablecloth will not <u>adequately</u> (adv.) cover the new dining room table, so we'll have to buy a bigger one.

2a. **apparent,** adj., clear, easy to see or understand

    It was <u>apparent</u> that everyone at the party liked the spicy noodles because they asked for more.

2b. **apparent,** adv., seemingly, according to what a person has seen or heard

    Finn was smiling and laughing, and he was <u>apparently</u> not worried that the pizza would arrive too late to serve at his party.

3. **assemble,** v.t., to put parts together to make something

    Before Jim begins to cook, he likes to <u>assemble</u> all the food and tools he needs in one place in the kitchen.

    When Ed bought a new grill, he made sure to buy one that said "no <u>assembly</u> (n.) required" on the box because he didn't want to put it together.

4. **calorie,** n., a unit to measure the energy that food produces

    A dinner of fried chicken, French fries, and cookies has more <u>calories</u> than a dinner of grilled fish, rice, salad, and an apple.

    A <u>caloric</u>-needs (adj.) calculator can tell you how much you should eat to maintain your weight.

5. **capacity,** n., the amount that something can hold or contain

   Maureen's dishwasher is very big. It has the <u>capacity</u> to wash 30 dishes and 15 glasses.

   Our office coffee pot has a 12-cup <u>capacity</u>.

6. **disgust,** v.t., to cause strong feelings of dislike

   The garbage next to the restaurant <u>disgusted</u> Steve and Debby, so they decided to eat somewhere else.

   What is <u>disgusting</u> (adj.) to one person may be delicious to another. For example, some international students think that apple pie is too sweet, but it's a very popular dessert in the United States.

7. **distinct,** adj., easy to notice; clear; different; separate

   Strawberries have a very <u>distinct</u> appearance. Connor can always find them quickly at the supermarket because of their bright red color.

   Ibrahim cannot make a <u>distinction</u> (n.) between types of apples unless they are different colors.

8. **flexible,** adj., able to change in new situations

   Frank is not very <u>flexible</u> when it comes to new recipes. He likes to make the same recipe again and again and does not want to try anything new.

   There is some <u>flexibility</u> (n.) in Sri's budget to buy imported ingredients from time to time.

9. **ingredient**, n., an item of food used to make something to eat or drink

Erik does not know much about cooking, so he likes to cook easy dishes with simple ingredients like chicken, noodles, onions, and carrots.

The main ingredient in this soup is garlic, and that's why it has such a strong aroma.

10. **means**, n., a way of doing something

My oven is broken, so I do not have the means to cook for my parents when they visit. I think I'll take them to a restaurant.

Is there a means of having groceries delivered to your home?

11. **nutritious**, adj., food that is good for your health

Many parents complain that school lunches are not very nutritious because they have too much fat and sugar in them.

Because hospital nutritionists (n.) must know a lot about planning healthy menus, many of them have a college degree in nutrition (n.).

12. **portion**, n., a measurement of food, usually for one person

When a fast food restaurant asks if a customer wants to get the "big" meal or the "super" meal, it is asking if the customer wants a larger portion.

When dividing food, we sometimes use the "I cut, you choose" method. Person A divides the food into two portions, and Person B chooses her portion first. This way, the portions are usually the same size.

13. **range**, n., variety; a collection of different types of things

In the past, people shopped at specialty stores like bakeries and produce markets for their food. Now, supermarkets offer such a range of foods and other items that specialty stores cannot always stay in business.

Carlo's favorite foods range (v.i.) from bananas to steak.

14. **raw**, adj., not cooked

Vegetables lose some of their nutrients during cooking, so it is usually healthier to eat raw vegetables.

Christine asked the waiter to take her steak back to the kitchen and have it cooked more because it was too raw.

15. **recipe**, n., instructions for making something to eat or drink

The recipe for chocolate chip cookies includes butter, brown sugar, flour, eggs, and semi-sweet chocolate chips.

I recommend following a recipe the first time that you make something new. After you know what the dish tastes like, you can make changes.

16. **regard**, v.t., to think of something or somebody in a particular way

Chefs regard cooking as a profession, not as a job or a hobby.

Chocolate from Belgium is regarded by many as some of the best in the world.

17. **reverse**, v.t., to move in the opposite way or direction

I ruined the cake I was making because I <u>reversed</u> the amount of sugar with the amount of flour.

We expected the restaurant to be very expensive, but it was just the <u>reverse</u> (n.). Although the food was excellent, the prices were reasonable.

18. **starve**, v.i., to suffer or die from a lack of food; to be very hungry

So many people around the world <u>starve</u> to death every year that we must find a solution to this important world issue.

According to some statistics, more than 15 million children die of <u>starvation</u> (n.) every year. Most of these children live in poor areas where growing food is difficult.

Vocabulary Practice

A. Make the Connection

Choose the vocabulary word that is most closely related to each sentence. The first one has been done as an example.

flexible	~~starvation~~	distinct
capacity	assembly	reversal
adequate	regard	nutrition

1. Thousands of people die each year because they do not have enough food to eat. _____ **starvation** _____

2. A healthy diet includes whole grains, vegetables, fruits, dairy, protein, and fats and sugars. _____

3. There is no stress when I invite Kylie for dinner because if I make a mistake cooking the meal, she does not mind going out to eat instead.

    _____

4. Ryan didn't like chicken before, but when I served roast chicken with lemon, he changed his mind completely. _____

5. We had just enough cupcakes for all of the children at the party.

    _____

6. I consider Yan to be a great friend as well as my cooking teacher.

    _____

7. My dad and brother bought the parts for a kitchen shelf and then put the parts together. _____

8. These two juices taste very different; one is sweet, the other is quite sour.

    _____

9. Rosie decided that she couldn't have the cookie baking party at her house because there was not enough space for all those people.

    _____

B. Switch It Up

Each sentence contains an incorrect form of the underlined vocabulary word. Write the appropriate form of the word in the blank. The first one has been done as an example.

1. _____*flexible*_____ When cooking at home, try to be very flexibility. Be creative, and just use whatever ingredients you have.

2. _____ The distinctly between fresh fish and frozen fish is remarkable, so Arlette only buys fresh fish.

3. _____ When my grandmother realized that she did not have an adequately number of paper plates for the picnic, she sent my grandfather to the store to buy more.

4. _____ Schools start to teach children about nutritious when they are young so that the children can develop healthy eating habits.

5. _____ Although I received an acceptance letter to cooking school, I was told that there had been a reverse of the decision and I was no longer accepted.

6. _____ When Ahmed saw all the trash in the classroom left by the other students, he was disgusting and disappointed.

7. _____ Nancy decoratively assembly the flowers around the wedding cake yesterday before the ceremony.

8. _____ Jeremy was so hungry after working out at the gym that he called his mother on the phone and asked her to heat up a pizza because he was <u>starvation</u>.

9. _____ The Chinatown Restaurant is <u>apparent</u> very popular. Look at the long lines!

10. _____ The <u>calorie</u> value of cakes and cookies is higher than the vitamins and minerals they provide.

C. In the Wrong Place

In each paragraph, the underlined vocabulary words are in the wrong place. Cross out the inappropriate word and replace it with the underlined word that makes sense. The first one has been done as an example.

1. Television food programs have become very popular in the United States. One program shows how everyday items that we eat are ~~ingredients~~ *assembled*. For example, the program may visit a factory where a particular candy bar is made. The program shows the machines that are used, the process for making the candy bars, and how all the ~~recipe~~ *ingredients* come together. Sometimes they even share the ~~assembled~~ *recipe*.

2. Markets come in many sizes. Some markets have a small number of specialty items, while others have a wide means_____ of products. Smaller markets often have to limit their selection because they have a very limited range_____ for storage. Larger markets often have the flexibility_____ to offer a wider selection and have the capacity_____ to add new products at any time. Because larger stores can buy in greater quantities, their prices may also be cheaper.

3. Mandy and Terry are trying to decide where to have dinner, which is difficult because they have very different tastes. Mandy wants to go for sushi, but Terry cannot stand the idea of anyone eating disgusts_____ fish. Terry wants to go to a steak house, but Mandy thinks that the raw_____ are too big and seeing so much food on one plate apparent_____ her. After discussing where to go for 30 minutes, no portions_____ can be found, so they decide to stay home and cook for themselves.

4. In many countries, lack of adequately_____ is a serious problem. It is caused when the food that people eat does not starving_____ nourish their bodies. For example, yams have more vitamins than rice and also fewer nutrition_____. If people ate yams instead of rice, they would be healthier. People who are calories_____ need to be given better food, as well as more food.

D. What's the Word?

With your partner, fill in each box on the grid. Student A will use Grid A. Student B will use Grid B in Appendix 1 on page 167. Each grid is missing different words. Describe the words on your grid so your partner can fill in his or her blank spaces. When all of the blanks are full, compare your grids to see if you have the correct answers.

> **Example:** For Box 1, Student B might give Student A these clues: *It's an adjective. It means easy to see or understand; a situation or a fact that is clear.*

Grid A

1	5 regard	9	13 flexible
2	6	10 adequate	14
3 disgusting	7 raw	11	15
4	8 range	12	16 caloric

Frequent Collocations: Food and Nutrition

Some common food and nutrition collocations are listed. What others can you think of?

1. **adequate**—adequate protection, an adequate supply, to provide adequate nutrition
2. **disgust**—an expression/feeling of disgust, to be filled with disgust, to be gross and disgusting
3. **distinct**—clearly distinct, a distinct advantage, quite/very distinct
4. **ingredient**—to be the essential/necessary/key ingredient
5. **nutritious**—to be highly nutritious, nutrition information
6. **portion**—a large/small portion, a greater portion of
7. **range**—a price range, within range, a wide range
8. **raw**—raw food, raw materials, raw meat
9. **recipe**—a favorite/secret recipe, to follow a recipe
10. **starve**—to let someone starve, to starve to death, starving children

E. Get It Together

Unscramble the words and phrases to write sentences containing the collocations. The first one has been done as an example.

1. delicious and / The dessert / was / highly / nutritious / fruity

   <u>**The fruity dessert was delicious and highly nutritious.**</u>

2. in the sauce / ingredient / is a key / Garlic / at Vito's pizza restaurant

   _____

   _____

3. shared / her secret / The cooking teacher / recipe / with the class / for pancakes

   _____

   _____

4. with disgust / can fill people / The idea of / eating insects

   _____

   _____

5. Happy Bob's Restaurant / large / portions, / but / kids loved it / did not sell

_____

_____

6. Does / of products? / offer / a wide / the new grocery store / range

_____

_____

7. meat / raw / Ali Baba's / is famous / for serving

_____

_____

8. children / We always / to organizations / donate money / that help starving

_____

_____

F. Not Meant To Be

These collocations are incorrect. Read all of the underlined words, and choose the one that best matches or collocates with the first word. Use the list of frequent collocations to help you. The first one has been done as an example.

1. ~~adequate~~ <u>ingredient</u>   *adequate supply*

2. nutrition <u>to death</u>   _____

3. price ~~supply~~   _____

4. essential <u>portion</u>   _____

5. filled <u>materials</u>   _____

6. starve <u>information</u>   _____

7. greater <u>range</u>   _____

8. raw <u>with disgust</u>   _____

Practice Quiz

G. The Choice Is Yours

Circle the best answer.

1. Nutritious food is _____.

    a. bad for your health

    b. good for your health

    c. expensive

    d. harmful

2. If you eat raw foods, you _____.

    a. pay a lot of money for them

    b. eat food from many countries

    c. buy them in restaurants

    d. do not cook them

3. If a restaurant is filled to capacity, then _____.

    a. no tables are available for new customers

    b. the customers are happy

    c. the workers know what to do

    d. the food is very expensive

4. Carola is trying to decrease her calorie intake, so she probably wants to _____.

   a. lose weight

   b. eat more

   c. gain weight

   d. eat the same amount

5. Many restaurants in the United States serve portions that are very _____.

   a. quiet

   b. starving

   c. large

   d. distinct

6. If you don't want to put a new kitchen table together, buy one that says _____.

   a. "clearly apparent"

   b. "low-calorie diet"

   c. "secret recipe"

   d. "no assembly required"

7. Starvation is a serious world problem because it causes many _____.

    a. accidents

    b. deaths

    c. alternatives

    d. doctors

8. The best place to find a good recipe is in a _____.

    a. cookbook

    b. dictionary

    c. comic book

    d. newspaper

9. If you plan a big dinner, be sure to buy all of the _____.

    a. hard recipes

    b. high calories

    c. essential ingredients

    d. disgusting food

10. The restaurant went out of business, so the owner had a _____.

    a. distinct advantages

    b. flexible schedule

    c. nutritious meals

    d. reversal of fortune

H. Sense or Nonsense?

Using your knowledge of the unit's target vocabulary, write Y (yes) for statements that make sense or N (no) for statements that do not make sense.

1. _____ If you are able to buy what you need, you have an adequate supply of money.

2. _____ Sally orders a chocolate dessert every time it is offered on a menu because she thinks that chocolate is disgusting.

3. _____ The taste of oranges and the taste of tangerines are quite distinct: one is sweet and the other is sour.

4. _____ If a cook buys excellent ingredients and follows a good recipe, she should make a delicious meal.

5. _____ If you regard food only as a means to stay alive, you usually love to cook.

6. _____ If the answer to a problem is apparent, you will have difficulty solving it.

7. _____ Restaurants that offer a wide range of vegetarian dishes have to buy a lot of meat.

8. _____ A nutritionist can help you if you have trouble paying for your lunch at a restaurant.

9. _____ If you do not have the means to eat at expensive restaurants, you should eat in them every night.

10. _____ If you do not make a reservation at a popular restaurant, you may have to be flexible about what time you eat.

Plants and Animals

Word Form Chart

Noun	Verb	Adjective	Adverb
confinement confines	**confine**	confined confining	
consciousness		**conscious** unconscious	consciously unconsciously
disturbance	**disturb**	disturbing	disturbingly
fragility		**fragile**	
maturity immaturity	mature	mature **immature**	maturely immaturely
inhabitant habitat	**inhabit**	inhabitable inhabited	
irritation irritant	**irritate**	irritable irritated irritating	
native		**native**	
pertinence	pertain	**pertinent**	pertinently
promotion	**promote**		
regulation	**regulate**	regulated	
resistance	**resist**	resistant resistible	
sensitivity		**sensitive**	sensitively
surroundings	surround	surrounded surrounding	
uniqueness		**unique**	uniquely
vegetation	vegetate	vegetative	
veterinarian		veterinary	

Definitions and Examples of Word Forms

1. **confine,** v.t., to keep someone or something within limited space; to limit actions

   These days, many people who get a puppy <u>confine</u> it in a crate for periods of time.

   If an animal is kept in close <u>confinement</u> (n.) for a long time, it can often become sick.

2. **conscious,** adj., to be aware of what is happening around you; to be awake

   In Rwanda, Mandy noticed that if she sat quietly for a length of time, the gorillas seemed less <u>conscious</u> of her presence.

   Tobias fell and hit his head when he was hiking in the woods. He lost <u>consciousness</u> (n.) for a few minutes, but the doctor says he'll be all right.

3. **disturb,** v.t., to interrupt; to bother or annoy someone or something; to cause anxiety

   John's dog Lady bit his uncle because he <u>disturbed</u> Lady while she was eating.

   It is <u>disturbing</u> (adj.) to me when my neighbor's dog barks all night.

4. **fragile,** adj., easily damaged or destroyed

   Eggshells are <u>fragile</u> and easily broken.

   When an animal is born, it needs to be protected and cared for. Because of its <u>fragility</u> (n.), the parents protect it until the baby animal is strong enough to take care of itself.

5. **immature**, adj., not fully developed or grown

   A cub is a young or immature bear or lion.

   Although my son is 14 years old, he is too immature to take good care of a pet. I have to remind him every day to feed our dog.

6. **inhabit**, v.t., to live in

   Bears commonly inhabit big forests because forests have the kind of shelter and food they need.

   Because a chemical company dumped poison into the river, all of the river's inhabitants (n.) have died.

7. **irritate**, v.t., to make uncomfortable in some way; to annoy

   Some plants, such as poison ivy, irritate the skin.

   My dog Kelso becomes irritable (adj.) when he is attacked by fleas.

8. **native**, adj., a plant, animal, or person that comes from a place

   Rice is believed to be native to Asia and was carried from there to other places in the world, such as Africa.

   Madagascar, an island off the coast of Africa, has many types of animals that are native to the island and exist nowhere else in the world, such as lemurs.

9. **pertinent**, adj., important or related to something

   Many people think that bulls respond to the color red. However, the color is not pertinent. It is actually movement that attracts the bull's attention.

   The pertinence (n.) of language to human evolution cannot be overstated.

10. **promote,** v.t., to help someone or something advance, develop, progress

In the tropics, hot, humid weather <u>promotes</u> the growth of orchids, a beautiful flower.

Smokey the Bear is a character used in the <u>promotion</u> (n.) of forest fire prevention.

11. **regulate,** v.t., to control an activity or process by making rules or laws; to control the rate of a process for proper operation

Sometimes governments try to <u>regulate</u> the movement of wildlife by building fences so that wildlife can't get into certain areas.

Animals produce hormones to <u>regulate</u> growth.

12. **resist,** v.t., to work against someone or something; ability to survive or overcome

The government's tax on growing corn was <u>resisted</u> by farmers.

Animals that are <u>resistant</u> (adj.) to bacterial infections are more likely to survive in the wilderness.

13. **sensitive,** adj., to notice and respond to changes quickly; aware of others' feelings; easily upset

Scientists have noticed that because frogs have thin skin, they are very <u>sensitive</u> to changes in the strength of sunlight.

Stefan's cat is <u>sensitive</u> to loud noises like thunder.

14. **surroundings**, n., area around people, animals, or things

If you live in urban <u>surroundings</u>, like a city, you may feel uncomfortable in a forest, especially at night.

The forest is <u>surrounded</u> (v.t.) by cities. This causes problems for both the animals in the forest and humans; the humans try to take more land from the forest and the animals try to take more land from the cities.

15. **unique**, adj., special; like no other

Elephants are precious because they are <u>unique</u>. There are no other animals like them in the world.

The platypus is <u>unique</u> because it is an animal that lays eggs like a reptile and feeds it babies with milk like a mammal.

16. **vegetation**, n., plants; plant material

Compared to rainforests, deserts are very dry places with little <u>vegetation</u>.

Animals like cows and horses eat mostly <u>vegetative</u> (adj.) matter; they don't eat meat.

17. **veterinarian**, n., a doctor of animal medicine

Becoming a <u>veterinarian</u> requires as much education as becoming a doctor for people.

<u>Veterinary</u> (adj.) services are very expensive in the United States. As a result, some people buy health insurance for their pets.

Vocabulary Practice

A. Match Point

Write the letter of the best definition next to each word. The first one has been done as an example.

1. __b__ vegetation

2. ____ unique

3. ____ surroundings

4. ____ sensitive

5. ____ resist

6. ____ promote

7. ____ irritate

8. ____ regulate

9. ____ pertinent

10. ____ fragile

11. ____ conscious

12. ____ confine

a. make known to others

b. greenery, plant life

c. relevant

d. limit someone's space or actions

e. one of a kind

f. overcome, survive

g. control with rules or laws

h. environment

i. quickly responds to the surroundings

j. delicate, easily harmed

k. annoy

l. aware of certain facts

B. Make the Connection

Choose the vocabulary word that is most closely related to each sentence.
The first one has been done as an example.

disturb	fragile	veterinarian
~~pertinent~~	resist	conscious
unique	vegetation	native

1. Natalia told her vet, Claudia, exactly what her sick dog ate.
   _____**pertinent**_____

2. There are areas on Earth, such as deserts and tundra, that have very little plant life. _____

3. Bai's horse will have her baby soon. We need to be sure there is medical help in case she has difficulty. _____

4. People need to become aware of their effect on the earth.

   _____

5. Bears cannot stay away from the food of campers. _____

6. Although the potato is a very important food in the northern parts of Europe, it originated in South America. _____

7. The Galapagos Islands have plants and animals that cannot be found anywhere else in the world. _____

8. Coral reefs, which are found in the Pacific and Indian Oceans, are very easily damaged. _____

9. Most people are afraid of snakes. But in my experience, if you don't bother them, they won't bother you. _____

C. Switch It Up

Each sentence contains an incorrect form of the underlined vocabulary word. Write the appropriate form of the word in the blank. The first one has been done as an example.

1. _____*irritable*_____ A person or animal that hasn't had enough to eat and sleep is often <u>irritation</u>.

2. _____ At first, it appears that no animals <u>inhabitable</u> the desert, but with observation, one can see that there are all sorts of wildlife there.

3. _____ If you hike in an area with poisonous snakes, you should wear boots that are <u>resistible</u> to snake bites.

4. _____ Walk quietly through the forest so that you don't <u>disturbance</u> the animals.

5. _____ A climate that is neither too cold nor too hot is <u>pertinence</u> to an animal's well-being.

6. _____ When flying a pet from one country to another, the animal must be <u>confinement</u> in a cage.

7. _____ Because many plants in the rainforest don't get a lot of sunlight, they are very <u>sensitivity</u> to too much sun.

8. _____ Julio sells the puppies even though they are too <u>immaturity</u> to leave their mothers to make money more quickly.

9. _____ The National Wildlife Federation <u>promotion</u> wildlife protection because some animals, like the wolf and polar bear, are in danger.

10. _____ The <u>veterinary</u> will operate on your dog's broken leg.

D. Off Base

The underlined word in each sentence does not make sense. Cross out each underlined word or phrase, and replace it with a vocabulary word from the unit that fits the context. You may have to change the verb form. The first one has been done as an example.

1. The village people who lived near the forest ~~easily accepted~~ **resisted** _____ the government's plan to relocate them because it changed every aspect of their lives.

2. Many plants have sharp parts that are <u>nice and soothing</u> _____ to touch.

3. Panda bears are <u>ordinary</u>_____ animals that eat only bamboo plants.

4. Animals that are <u>fully developed</u> _____ need some help to survive.

5. The bald eagle is <u>not original</u>_____ to North America.

6. I was <u>not aware   </u> of the sign on the Hawaiian beach that tells people to keep a distance from the sea turtles, so I didn't touch them.

7. The outer covering of eggs offer some protection even though that covering is <u>strong   </u>.

8. Because of the increasing human population, wildlife issues need to be <u>uncontrolled   </u>.

9. Human beings as well as animals are affected by their <u>internal states   </u> and suffer when they live in poor conditions.

10. Since Zeynep's skin is very<u> tough   </u>, she must be careful not to touch any unknown plants when she walks in the forest.

Frequent Collocations: Plants and Animals

Some common plants and animals collocations are listed. What others can you think of?

1. **confine**—beyond the confines of, outside the confines of, within the confines of
2. **conscious**—to make a conscious decision/effort, to be environmentally conscious
3. **inhabit**—a habitat of [a certain species], a loss of habitat, a wildlife habitat
4. **pertinent**—pertinent information, pertinent questions, to be especially/particularly pertinent
5. **promote**—to promote development, to promote growth, promotion efforts/programs
6. **regulate**—environmental regulations, government regulations, to have the authority to regulate
7. **resist**—to meet with resistance, resistance to disease, a resistance movement
8. **sensitive**—to be very/highly sensitive, a sensitive issue, to be environmentally sensitive
9. **unique**—a unique experience, a unique opportunity, to have unique needs/characteristics
10. **vegetation**—dense vegetation, native vegetation, soil for vegetation

E. Not Meant To Be

These collocations are incorrect. Read all of the underlined words, and choose the one that best matches or collocates with the first word. Use the list of frequent collocations to help you. The first one has been done as an example.

1. ~~pertinent~~ effort   *pertinent questions* _____

2. native <u>movement</u>   _____

3. unique ~~questions~~   _____

4. promote <u>regulations</u>   _____

5. resistance <u>vegetation</u>   _____

6. environmental <u>growth</u>   _____

7. conscious <u>habitat</u>   _____

8. wildlife <u>needs</u>   _____

F. Stick Like Glue

Pair the vocabulary words in boldface with the appropriate collocates in the word bank. The first one has been done as an example.

authority to	1. resistance to	2. conscious	3. unique	4. pertinent
environmentally	5. habitat	particularly	outside the	6. promotion
7. confines of	effort	8. regulate	9. vegetation	dense
opportunity	10. sensitive	disease	loss of	efforts

1. <u>resistance to disease</u>

2. _____

3. _____

4. _____

5. _____

6. _____

7. _____

8. _____

9. _____

10. _____

Practice Quiz

G. The Choice Is Yours

Circle the best answer.

1. The vegetation in the forest refers to _____.

   a. dead leaves

   b. green plant life

   c. animals

   d. soil

2. Elephants are native to Africa meaning they _____.

   a. were brought to Africa a long time ago

   b. used to be from another place

   c. are originally from Africa

   d. come from specific parts of Africa

3. Chad disturbed the bird's nest by _____.

   a. telling his friend about it

   b. not knowing about it

   c. looking at it

   d. moving it

4. The Kenyan government regulated the selling of ivory, so the sale of ivory _____.

   a. increased

   b. stayed the same

   c. became free

   d. was controlled

5. Zoos have improved the surroundings provided to the animals so _____.

   a. the quality of the food is better

   b. the health care given to the animals is better

   c. the spaces the animals live in are larger

   d. the animal shows people can see are funnier

6. Chimpanzees are not sensitive to the AIDS virus, which means that they _____.

   a. develop violent symptoms of the virus

   b. are not aware of the virus

   c. do not react to the virus

   d. react to the virus

7. A veterinarian works with ____.

   a. horses and dogs

   b. plants and fungi

   c. men and women

   d. plants and animals

8. Duckbilled platypuses are unique and ____.

   a. they are very common

   b. there is no other animal like them

   c. they come from many places

   d. they can be trained

9. An immature dog ____.

   a. behaves very well

   b. is always playful

   c. is not fully developed

   d. is ten years old

10. If a lion has to be confined, it ____.

   a. is restricted to a certain area

   b. has to eat only certain foods

   c. is living in the jungle

   d. needs veterinary help

H. Sense or Nonsense?

Using your knowledge of the unit's target vocabulary, write Y (yes) for statements that make sense or N (no) for statements that do not make sense.

1. _____   Water is irritating to all living things.

2. _____   To protect native species, governments sometimes restrict the types of plants and animals that are permitted into a country.

3. _____   Some people's skin is sensitive to certain plant substances.

4. _____   If you want to catch fish, the type of bait you use is pertinent.

5. _____   Australia is known for the animals that inhabit that country, like the kangaroo and the koala bear.

6. _____   For hundreds of years, humans were not conscious of the need to protect the environment.

7. _____   A newborn animal is usually mature in the first few days or weeks of life.

8. _____   Flowers that are fragile like orchids can grow in any climate.

9. _____   There are no organizations that promote the importance of animals.

10. _____   Kari studied astrophysics because she is concerned about her surroundings.

Unit **8**

Science

Word Form Chart

Noun	Verb	Adjective	Adverb
analysis analyst	**analyze**	analytic analytical	analytically
concept conception	conceptualize conceive	conceptual	conceptually
concrete		**concrete**	concretely
consistency		**consistent**	consistently
dimension		dimensional	
emission	**emit**		
hypothesis	hypothesize	hypothetical	hypothetically
illumination	**illuminate**	illuminated	
inquiry inquirer	**inquire**	inquisitive	inquisitively
invisibility		**invisible**	invisibly
pioneer	pioneer	pioneering	
pressure	pressure	pressured	
radiation	**radiate**		
rotation	**rotate**	rotating	
spark	spark		
synthesis	synthesize		
theory theorist	theorize	theoretical	theoretically
tube			

Definitions and Examples

1. **analyze,** v.t., to study something closely in order to understand it

    The chemists at Environmental Services, Inc., <u>analyzed</u> the water to see if it was clean and fit to drink.

    NASA's <u>analysis</u> (n.) of these photos from the space telescope shows that the surface of Mars may be colder than we thought.

2. **concept,** n., a complex or original idea; a model for scientific thinking

    About 500 years ago, the astronomer Copernicus developed the <u>concept</u> of a solar system where the Earth and other planets move around the sun.

    Charles Darwin <u>conceptualized</u> (v.t.) how living things could evolve over many years and create new species.

3. **concrete,** adj., can be touched or seen; real

    Good scientists won't accept new theories until they are supported by <u>concrete</u> evidence and observations.

    The biologists at our university described the kind of laboratory they want, and now the engineers and architects have to think <u>concretely</u> (adv.) about how they might build such a lab.

4. **consistent,** adj., happening regularly in the same way; producing the same results

    The results of our second experiment were <u>consistent</u> with the results of the first one, and that confirmed our belief that the first one was done correctly.

    Professor Martin's solar panels needed to produce cheap energy <u>consistently</u> (adv.) and reliably every time she used them before she could sell them to the public.

5. **dimension,** n., one side of a shape or object; the size or dimensions of an object or area

   A circle drawn on paper has only two <u>dimensions</u> (length and height), but a sphere has three (length, height, and depth).

   Microbiologists need powerful microscopes to study bacteria and other organisms of very small <u>dimensions</u>.

6. **emit,** v.t., to send out energy or sound; to let out a gas or liquid

   Radio stations <u>emit</u> radio waves that can be captured by radio antennae and converted to sound.

   Today, in California and many other states, automobiles are tested for the amount of <u>emissions</u> (n.) they make into the air, and a car can be taken off the road if it produces too much pollution.

7. **hypothesis,** n., an idea that has not yet been proven or disproven

   In the late 1400s, there was a <u>hypothesis</u> that the Earth was round, but people weren't sure until Magellan's ship sailed all the way around the world.

   Some scientists <u>hypothesize</u> (v.t.) that man-made pollution will warm our planet by several degrees Celsius over the next century.

8. **illuminate,** v.t., to shine light on an object to make it bright or to see it better

   The Sun <u>illuminates</u> half of Earth's surface at a time while the other half is in darkness.

   Almost no light reaches the deepest parts of the ocean, but some fish who live there have special glands that produce their own <u>illumination</u> (n.).

9. **inquire**, v.t., v.i., to ask questions about something; to investigate a topic or problem

   Marie and Pierre Curie were famous scientists who <u>inquired</u> into the nature of radioactivity and how it might be applied to medicine.

   Good researchers have to be <u>inquisitive</u> (adj.) and curious about the branch of science they study.

10. **invisible**, adj., not capable of being seen by the human eye

    Radio waves are all around, but they're <u>invisible</u>.

    The <u>invisibility</u> (n.) of the air we breathe makes it difficult to understand the complexity of the atmosphere and all the layers that are in it.

11. **pioneer**, n., someone who makes important discoveries before other people

    Edwin Hubble was a <u>pioneer</u> in the fields of astronomy and cosmology, and many scientists have studied and admired his work.

    In the Middle Ages, scientists in the Arab world <u>pioneered</u> (v.t.) the study of chemistry and medicine, and Europeans later copied what they had done.

12. **pressure**, n., the force or stress from one thing pushing against another

    Oceanographers and marine biologists have to wear special protective diving suits when they go deep under the sea because the water <u>pressure</u> is so great that it would crush them otherwise.

    Diamonds are formed when carbon is buried deep underground and <u>pressured</u> (v.t.) into a new form by the tremendous weight of many tons of rock and dirt.

13. **radiate,** v.t., v.i., to send out light, heat, or other forms of energy

    The Sun <u>radiates</u> heat throughout the solar system, and a small amount of that heat warms Earth and makes life possible here.

    People who work with nuclear power must be careful because too much <u>radiation</u> (n.) from uranium can make them sick or kill them.

14. **rotate,** v.t., v.i., to move in a circular motion around an object or central point; to revolve or spin

    The moon <u>rotates</u> around the Earth about once a month, and the Earth <u>rotates</u> around the Sun once a year.

    In an automobile, energy is produced in the engine and transferred to the crank shafts, which are long poles that cause the <u>rotation</u> (n.) of the wheels.

15. **spark,** n., a small, brief flash of fire or electrical energy; anything that activates or stimulates

    Be careful: There is so much pure oxygen in this laboratory that even a small <u>spark</u> can cause an explosion.

    The scientist presented a theory that is certain to <u>spark</u> (v.t.) further research.

16. **synthesis,** n., a mixture of two or more substances; a combination of objects or ideas

    Read Amy Brown's paper, which contains a <u>synthesis</u> of the existing theories about how language originated.

    Thanks to advances in audio science, we can <u>synthesize</u> (v.t.) music electronically and make it sound very much like real music made by musicians.

17. **theory,** n., an idea about how things or processes work; a framework for explaining scientific facts

    According to Einstein's <u>Theory</u> of Relativity, nothing in the universe can travel faster than light.

    Charles Darwin <u>theorized</u> (v.t.) that modern animals and plants had evolved from earlier, simpler forms, and today most biologists agree that he was correct.

18. **tube,** n., a long, round device used to hold or transport liquids or gases

    Dr. LeClerc drew a blood sample from the sick man, put it in a <u>tube</u>, sealed it, and sent it to the laboratory to be examined.

    Oxygen moves through the <u>tubes</u> in the machine to a small tank, where it is mixed with other gases.

Vocabulary Practice

A. Make the Connection

Choose the vocabulary word that is most closely related to each sentence. The first one has been done as an example.

emit	hypothesis	inquiry
synthesis	concrete	pressure
tube	pioneer	spark

1. Light and sound travel through the air in a way similar to ripples of water in the ocean. _____ *emit* _____

2. Scientists have two different materials that can be combined to form a stronger, more flexible material. _____

3. Because my son has a lot of questions about how things work, I encourage him to investigate. _____

4. New fossils have been found in South Africa that shed light on when Neanderthal culture began. _____

5. Spaceships must be strong enough to maintain their shape in a vacuum. _____

6. The chemistry department orders a lot of glass things for their experiments. _____

7. The first men on the moon felt very much like the first people to visit a new continent. _____

8. Scientists think abstractly, but they must be able to prove their theories using real evidence. _____

9. Halle caused a controversy in scientific circles with his new theory about the origin of life on Mars. _____

B. Switch It Up

Each sentence contains an incorrect form of the underlined vocabulary word. Write the appropriate form of the word in the blank. The first one has been done as an example.

1. _____**conceptualize**_____ Great scientists can often <u>concept</u> an idea before they can prove it is true.

2. _____ After finishing the experiment, John did the <u>analyze</u>.

3. _____ The institute will not give Xin funding unless she explains her ideas <u>concrete</u>.

4. _____ Physicists <u>theory</u> that dark matter is made up of tiny particles called the Higgs boson, but they need more proof.

5. _____ The <u>rotate</u> of the planets is caused by the Sun's gravitational pull.

6. _____ B. F. Skinner was a <u>pioneered</u> in the field of experimental psychology.

7. _____ To provide support for your theory, you must test a <u>hypothesize</u>.

8. _____ Does a black hole <u>emission</u> anything?

9. _____ The fabric of the universe is <u>invisibility</u>.

10. _____ Science strives to <u>illumination</u> the mysteries of nature.

C. In the Wrong Place

In each paragraph, the underlined vocabulary words are in the wrong place. Cross out the inappropriate word and replace it with the underlined word that makes sense. The first one has been done as an example.

1. Dr. Chen is an astronomer and he is also interested in the origins of life. He has an interesting ~~sparked~~ *hypothesis* that life originated outside of Earth and was brought here by meteors. He believes that some of the meteors that have crashed to the Earth show evidence of simple life forms that were so small they were ~~analyze~~ *invisible*. These small creatures probably ~~invisible~~ *sparked* bacterial life, which eventually became plants and animals, according to Dr. Chen. He wants to find more meteors and ~~hypothesis~~ *analyze* them to see if they provide further proof for his idea.

2. Good scientific researchers need several personality traits. First, they must be able to distinguish between inquisitive_____, which is only an idea, and fact, which has been proven. Second, they should be consistent_____ and conduct experiments that can either prove or disprove those ideas. Third, a good researcher has to repeat his or her experiments to show that the results will be synthesize_____ every time, not a matter of mere chance or luck. Finally, it helps if a researcher understands other people's research and can theory_____ information from various sources into new, original theories.

3. Stars <u>emit_____</u> as they move through space, and
    as they make this spinning motion they <u>rotate_____</u>
    huge amounts of heat and light, which reach all of the planets in
    their orbits. The heat energy is <u>illumination_____</u>
    to the human eye. The light, however, provides the
    <u>invisible_____</u> that makes our sense of sight possible.

4. The field of physics is a very broad one that includes all sorts of
    issues. A <u>sparks_____</u> in this field sometimes
    <u>concrete_____</u> religious or moral debate. Even
    though physicists have <u>hypothesis_____</u> theories
    about the origins of life, it is very difficult for them to get
    <u>pioneered_____</u> proof.

D. What's the Word?

With your partner, fill in each box on the grid. Student A will use Grid A. Student B will use Grid B in Appendix 1 on page 168. Each grid is missing different words. Describe the words on your grid so your partner can fill in his or her blank spaces. When all of the blanks are full, compare your grids to see if you have the correct answers.

> **Example:** For Box 1, Student A could give Student B these clues: *It's a verb. Scientists do this to test their ideas. It is a guess about how things work.*

Grid A

1 theorize	5	9 emit	13 consistently
2	6 conceptual	10 spark	14
3	7 radiate	11	15 inquiry
4 dimension	8	12	16 pioneer

Frequent Collocations: Science

Some common science collocations are listed. What others can you think of?

1. **analyze**—to conduct an analysis, data analysis, statistical analysis
2. **concept**—an abstract concept, a conceptual framework/model, to develop a conceptual model, whole concept
3. **consistent**—consistent findings, consistent results, to be consistent with
4. **emit**—carbon/greenhouse emissions, to emit light, to reduce emissions
5. **hypothesis**—a null hypothesis, to support a hypothesis, to test a hypothesis
6. **inquire**—to inquire about/into, to inquire whether, scientific inquiry
7. **invisible**—almost/nearly invisible, highly/clearly visible, visible light
8. **pioneer**—to help pioneer, pioneering research, pioneering work
9. **pressure**—high pressure, to put pressure on, under pressure
10. **theory**—to be theoretically based/grounded, theory and practice, theory of relativity

E. Not Meant To Be

These collocations are incorrect. Read all of the underlined words, and choose the one that best matches or collocates with the first word. Use the list of frequent collocations to help you. The first one has been done as an example.

1. ~~data~~ about   _data analysis_

2. conceptual pioneer   _____

3. consistent invisible   _____

4. greenhouse framework   _____

5. support and practice   _____

6. inquire ~~analysis~~   _____

7. nearly a hypothesis   _____

8. help emissions   _____

9. under findings   _____

10. theory pressure   _____

F. Get It Together

Unscramble the words and phrases to write sentences containing the collocations. The first one has been done as an example.

1. scientists usually/ To answer / an analysis / conduct / questions

   <u>To answer questions, scientists usually conduct an</u>

   <u>analysis.</u>

2. his patients' cases / Freud developed / by looking at / his conceptual models / some of

   _____

   _____

3. to be reliable / If an experiment / it is considered / results / has consistent

   _____

   _____

4. emissions / reduce greenhouse / To stop global warming / we have to

   _____

   _____

5. a hypothesis / After developing / a researcher / must test / a theory,

   _____

   _____

6. inquiry / our understanding / has advanced / Scientific / of the world

_____

_____

7. is transformed into / Carbon / under intense / diamonds / when it is put / pressure

_____

_____

8. Einstein / of relativity / his theory / is famous for

_____

_____

Practice Quiz

G. The Choice Is Yours

Circle the best answer.

1. Pioneering work in a field of science is ____.

    a. new and creative

    b. old and repetitive

    c. easy to conduct

    d. worse than previous work

2. If Paul's results are consistent with Marie's, his results are ____.

    a. different from Marie's results

    b. similar to or the same as Marie's results

    c. better than Marie's results

    d. copied from Marie

3. An object that rotates ____.

    a. is hot

    b. spins or orbits

    c. moves upward

    d. is broken

4. If Professor McCabe makes a hypothesis, she _____.

     a. is probably in serious trouble

     b. has a detailed plan

     c. should see a doctor soon

     d. proposes an idea that may be tested

5. A laboratory that is illuminated well is _____.

     a. bright

     b. plain

     c. roomy

     d. comfortable

6. A scientist who analyzes a subject well will _____.

     a. change it completely

     b. strongly disagree with it

     c. understand it thoroughly

     d. not be able to explain it to others

7. A two-dimensional shape _____.

     a. is very large

     b. is impossible

     c. has width and height

     d. is arranged from worst to best

8. Atoms must be viewed with a microscope because otherwise they are _____.

   a. rotation

   b. spark

   c. tube

   d. invisible

9. The particle accelerator caused a spark at the facility, which _____.

   a. created a theory

   b. started a fire

   c. illuminated the city

   d. made it rain

10. John built a light-emitting diode, which _____.

   a. could shine for six hours

   b. could swallow all the light in the room

   c. worked when there was enough sunlight

   d. was only a hypothesis

H. Sense or Nonsense?

Using your knowledge of the unit's target vocabulary, write Y (yes) for statements that make sense or N (no) for statements that do not make sense.

1. _____ The lab assistant poured the liquid into a glass tube about six inches long.

2. _____ The sun's radiation can be used to heat houses and cook food.

3. _____ Hadiya found a way to synthesize a heat-resistant material from a plant that she found growing in a rain forest.

4. _____ Johann is the best theorist in our laboratory because he always cleans the lab thoroughly and makes sure that we have enough new equipment.

5. _____ The small submarine dived too deeply under the surface of the ocean and was crushed by the intense water pressure.

6. _____ Miranda is a successful research chemist who isn't very inquisitive about or interested in science.

7. _____ The dimensions of space are so huge that they're measured in light years.

8. _____ Julio is a consistent researcher. His work varies greatly in quality.

9. _____ Paul enjoys thinking conceptually about evolution. He only spends time on observing and recording small physical changes in living things.

10. _____ Drs. Chao and Ang did concrete work in physics. They worked on a mathematical formula for months without eating or sleeping.

Appendix 1:
Grid Bs for What's the Word?

Unit 1

Grid B

1	5 incentive	9	13 invest
2 deduction	6	10 conduct	14
3	7 specify	11	15
4 violate	8	12 compromise	16 optimize

Unit 2

Grid B

1	5 epidemic	9	13 fatally
2 infection	6	10 symptom	14
3	7 menace	11	15 healing
4 allergic	8	12 sibling	16

Unit 3

Grid B

1	5 horizontal	9	13 whistle
2 referee	6 prominent	10	14 glancing
3	7	11 reputation	15
4 dedicated	8	12 fairness	16 energetic

Unit 5

Grid B

1	5 contemporary	9	13
2 versatile	6	10	14 transparent
3 symmetrical	7	11 ultimate	15 synthetic
4	8 pale	12 restrict	16

Unit 6

Grid B

1 apparent	5	9 distinct	13
2 means	6 assembly	10	14 nutritious
3	7	11 portion	15 reverse
4 starving	8	12 capacity	16

Unit 8

Grid B

1	5 tube	9	13
2 analyze	6	10	14 synthesize
3 illumination	7	11 rotate	15
4	8 concrete	12 pressure	16

Appendix 2: Vocabulary List

The target vocabulary forms for each unit are listed.

1: Business

acquisition
asset
brief
capital
compensate/
   compensate (for)
compromise
conduct
deduct
export
found
incentive
invest
irrelevant
mutual
optimistic
personnel
specify
violate

2: Health

allergy
diagnose
epidemic
fatal
grief
heal
infection
injection
menace
mood
mortal
recur
sibling
sympathize
symptom
vision
wound

3: Sports

challenge
controversy
dedicated
energy
fair
fierce
glance
grip
horizontal
intense
league
persist
prominent
referee
reputation
rival
tournament
whistle

4: Transportation	**5: Fashion**	**6: Food and Nutrition**
abandon	contemporary	adequate
access	fascinate	apparent/apparently
anticipate	flaw	assemble
circumstances	glow	calorie
crucial	medium/media	capacity
entitle	pale	disgust
fare	precede	distinct
gear	restrict	flexible
impact	ridiculous	ingredient
interrupt	rip	means
mobile	stain	nutritious
parallel	symmetrical	portion
peak	synthetic	range
pilot	transparent	raw
situation	ultimate	recipe
steep	versatile	regard
undergo	vivid	reverse
urban		starve

7: Plants and Animals

confine

conscious

disturb

fragile

immature

inhabit

irritate

native

pertinent

promote

regulate

resist

sensitive

surroundings

unique

vegetation

veterinarian

8: Science

analyze

concept

concrete

consistent

dimension

emit

hypothesis

illuminate

inquire

invisible

pioneer

pressure

radiate

rotate

spark

synthesis

theory

tube